LEADERSHIP
PURE AND SIMPLE

LEADERSHIP PURE AND SIMPLE

How Transformative Leaders
Create Winning Organizations

David Wilkins
Greg Carolin

New York   Chicago   San Francisco   Lisbon   London   Madrid
Mexico City   Milan   New Delhi   San Juan   Seoul
Singapore   Sydney   Toronto

1 2 3 4 5 6 7 8 9 10   DOC/DOC   1 8 7 6 5 4 3 2

ISBN 978-0-07-179182-3
MHID 0-07-179182-5

e-ISBN 978-0-07-179183-0
e-MHID 0-07-179183-3

McGraw-Hill books are available at special quantity discounts to use as premiums and sales promotions or for use in corporate training programs. To contact a representative, please e-mail us at bulksales@ mcgraw-hill.com.

This book is printed on acid-free paper.

Contents

PART 4

THE LEADER AS SITUATION MANAGER

PART 5

THE LEADER AS PROCESS COACH AND MANAGER

PART 6

THE TRANSFORMATIONAL LEADER

Foreword

Over 35 years ago I asked myself a question: "Why is it that some organizations are consistently and repeatedly more successful than others?"

As the founder, I started our firm Decision Processes International (DPI). Fast-forward to today. Thousands of our clients around the world benefit from and continue to assist the team in developing the *critical thinking processes* we created from our discoveries. The DPI team and I invite you now to share in these discoveries.

You may think that it would be a very easy exercise to conclude that these organizations had great leaders and then try to characterize what personal attributes these leaders had. Heaven knows, countless authors have done similarly since. Fortunately, these fuzzy answers did not satisfy my intellect, nor did they pass muster to deep critical inspection.

Convinced that there was no mysterious magic behind the success of these firms, my team and I were determined to identify the tangible ingredients that led to their success.

The establishment of DPI as a global consulting organization, with me at the helm as founding partner, followed. The DPI partners around the world have been using and improving these critical thinking processes, working with over 1,000 company executives and their management teams, since 1978.

Although I didn't realize it at the time, my journey was one of leadership. In studying the thousands of clients, and the work of even more of their leaders, the DPI team and I managed to capture the essence of what it is that makes effective leaders. We managed to identify the critical thinking skills that made great leaders great.

More than that, we managed to codify these critical thinking skills so that anyone can easily practice them, in the form of three specific and fully describable processes these great leaders followed but were largely unaware of.

Of course, the world is a very different place today than it was in 1978 when I started my quest. However, here is an inescapable fact: great thinking never goes out of fashion. The winners in the marketplace are still those that can out-think, not out-muscle, their competitors. The need for critical thinking skills is as real today as it was then.

Indeed, the critical thinking processes I uncovered remain the bedrock of the transformational work DPI brings to our clients. Unlike advisory consultants who "tell" their clients what to do, we are a consulting firm with a difference: we bring critical thinking processes that help leaders—and their followers—to think more clearly, cohesively, and creatively.

Now, 35 years after I started this journey, I am delighted that David and Greg are sharing its continuation. It truly is *Leadership Pure and Simple: How Transformative Leaders Create Winning Organizations.*

Good reading!

—Michel Robert

Acknowledgments

We would like to acknowledge Michel (Mike) Robert for his years of perseverance in relentlessly searching for the answer to "Why is it that some organizations are consistently and repeatedly more successful than others?"

Mike and the original founding partners Michel Moisan and Craig Bowers, and Andrew Sng, who joined them very soon thereafter, developed a number of *critical thinking processes* in search of the answers to this question. To that team we say thank you for the years of developing, testing, refining, and implementing the processes discussed in this book. As we have worked with this team over the last decade, we have realized the unbelievable passion the team has for making a difference and the drive for helping organizations find opportunities to build leadership skills in their industries and drive success. Mike would acknowledge that his journey wouldn't have been possible without Ellie's support over the last 35 years, and we also recognize her contribution.

We owe particular debt to regional founding partners Andrew Sng and Rex Glanville for their instrumental role in developing us as critical thinkers and consultants. They continue to be wonderful role models of humble success, a never-ending source of inspiration, and mentors who also know that there is always something new to learn or to offer. We vividly recall Rex's powerful advocacy of this book and its underlying premise, a "dangerous" proposition when combined with our blissful ignorance of authorship! Rex's persistent and tenacious assistance in framing the content, and his reading and rereading of the draft content, has been instrumental in the wonderful result you now hold.

To Rachael, Hannah, Abigail, and Kirsten, thank you for the support you have given David over the years as a partner at DPI Asia, for those days and nights when he was away from home running projects with clients and the time researching and writing this book. To his parents, thank you for encouraging him to examine everything critically from an early age.

To the Carolin family and Oriel Willemse for the support you have given Greg over the last decade in his endeavor and quest to help companies improve their standing and competitiveness in their chosen markets. Your patience and support cannot be expressed in words more than Thank You!

To our clients around the globe, with whom DPI partners have worked over the last 35 years, thank you for allowing DPI to bring the critical thinking processes into your organizations, to assist you and your management teams to seek ways to *consistently and repeatedly be more successful than others in your industry.*

LEADERSHIP PURE AND SIMPLE

PART 1

TIMELESS LEADERSHIP IN A CHANGING WORLD

CHAPTER 1

The World in 2020

The world today is experiencing change of unprecedented speed and scope. And you don't need to be a historian to know that some organizations cope with, or indeed flourish from, change better than others. And you don't need exceptional foresight to know that the ability to handle change is going to be required more acutely in the future. This will be what separates the true leader from the rest of the pack.

Transformative leaders will require fundamental skills of leadership. An effective leader must be able to uncover and drive insight from changes specific to his or her industry and the world at large, translate this insight into an operable and sustainable strategy, underpin it with innovation, and drive it to conclusion through relentless, hard-nosed operational implementation. In our view this is Leadership, Pure and Simple. Regrettably, such skills are not as pervasive as one might expect. But they can be learned or acquired. That's why we wrote this book.

Confronted by change, the first question to be answered by any leader is, "Where are we going?" This question is becoming increasingly more difficult to answer. Or is it?

During one of his final lectures, Peter Drucker, the founder of modern management thinking, was asked, "Professor Drucker, you seem to have this incredible ability to predict the future. How do you do that?" To which he replied, "I cannot do that. What I do is to look out of the window and see things that others do not see."

So how can one gain more insight through one's own window into the future? Some research will help.

One trove of observations and foresight is the excellent Future Agenda open insight initiative led by Vodafone, the largest provider of mobile communications in Europe and Africa. This ambitious project convened collaborations of experts in a wide range of business, scientific, and economic disciplines to assemble a broad view of possible futures around the world. Many of the trends uncovered by the Future Agenda project and described in the organization's report *The World in 2020* have often cropped up during our client assignments. Here is some of what we see.

THE FOUR CERTAINTIES

Peering out through the window of the future can be a daunting task if one doesn't know where to look. The first things to look for are future certainties that can be clearly separated from speculative events. *Future certainties* are trends in which "the train has left the station" and the destination is known and is virtually certain. Obvious examples are the rise of China and India as political and economic powers. Other examples are changing demographics, such as developed nations getting "older" and developing nations getting "younger." According to Future Agenda, there will be four *macro certainties* developing in the next decade:

- A continued imbalanced population growth
- More key resource constraints
- An accelerating Asia wealth shift
- The achievement of universal data access

TEN BROAD TRENDS

The next level of inquiry can be built around these certainties. In our view the following 10 broad trends will impact almost all industries and organizations on the planet.

TREND 1. WEALTH CREATION

Future Agenda has described it this way: "How wealth is created, valued, shared, and used over the next decade is subject to a number of possible changes."

We agree. Powered by globalization, an unstoppable yet not fully understood force, previously unseen methods and centers of wealth creation will emerge. One could argue that the wealth creators of recent history were the Europeans (Industrial Revolution) followed by the United States (the American Century). There are clear signs that this is changing. China, India, and other emerging markets are operating on new definitions of *capitalism* that make hefty research and development investment more palatable. So-called *state capitalism* is characterized by state-owned or family-controlled firms that don't have the short-term, "beat the analyst forecasts" mentality of their Western counterparts. In the future, leaders will no longer be able to plan without considering the longer-term global marketplace.

Continuing its analysis, the Future Agenda proceeds:

> Globalization has connected many of us in ways we never conceived of, that allow new ideas to be shared and innovations to accelerate. It has also linked us together in ways that mean shocks in one region can quickly be transferred to another. A "flatter" world is providing opportunities for those with talent to leapfrog ahead of others, but at the same time there is a growing imbalance between the haves and the have-nots in society.

> The next decade will see new technologies that will
> drive new business models that will, in turn, change
> how wealth is created and shared, but it will also see
> political and social needs drive other changes in how
> we manage and use the wealth and resources that
> we have available. There is also a clearly significant
> influence in this area from the certain shift in the center
> of gravity to Asia and the consequences that this will
> have for wealth creation, trading and even currencies.

Which raises the question: What will be the specific impacts of these macro wealth creation trends on the outlook of your industry?

TREND 2. WEALTH DISTRIBUTION

The wealth gap between the rich and poor will continue to expand, fueled by widening differences in wealth between and within urban and rural communities. But, predicts Future Agenda, the rich and poor will still need each other:

> In recent years the gap between richer and poorer
> households has widened in most areas of the world despite
> strong economic growth that has created millions of jobs.
> This has applied not only in the gaps between some
> rich countries and some poor ones but also within many
> nations. The rich/poor gap in the United States has
> increased, just as it has in Brazil, India, and Africa.

We would agree with many in saying that urbanization is perhaps the most significant issue. However, there are no clear signs of governments making significant changes to taxation and spending policies to redress the imbalance. Access to good education will remain the catalyst to breaking through the divide. One analyst put it bluntly: "If it was simply a matter of robbing

Peter to give to Paul, humanity would have solved it [wealth redistribution] years ago."

According to Future Agenda, "Over the next decade, the gap between the haves and the have-nots will grow, even though there will be ever more interdependence, in some areas, between wealth-generation across the social spectrum."

One of the early authorities to recognize the wealth gap was C. K. Prahalad. In his book *The Fortune at the Bottom of the Pyramid*, he asks how this gap can potentially be closed or addressed. Prahalad ponders the question of "why we cannot create inclusive capitalism, and why all of our technology, managerial know-how and investment capacity cannot make even a minor contribution to the problem of pervasive global poverty and disenfranchisement." He then suggests that "refining developmental aid, subsidies, governmental support, reliance on deregulation and privatization of public assets, and the solutions of localized nongovernmental organizations (NGOs) is important, but it has not redressed the problem of poverty." Prahalad asks, "Why can't we mobilize the investment capacity of large firms with the knowledge and commitment of NGOs and the communities that need help?" Searching for unique solutions led him on a journey to understand and motivate organizations to imagine and act on their role in creating a more just and humane society.

The Fortune at the Bottom of the Pyramid does not look to answer the debates raging over whether globalization is good or bad or whether small or large corporations can tackle problems more efficiently. Instead, it focuses on what works, and it suggests ways that NGOs, domestic organizations, multinational corporations, governments, and even the poor themselves, through entrepreneurial activities, can come together and work to solve the problem of poverty and the growing divide between rich and poor.

Whether such collaboration is possible is open to question. Grameen Bank, the microcredit organization founded by

Mohammed Yunus, appeared to have hit the magic formula and earned Yunus fame and a Nobel Prize along the way. However, recent criticisms leveled against Grameen in the Norwegian television documentary *Caught in Micro Debt* and controversies over the role and benefits of other microcredit organizations in other developing nations have been a setback. Nevertheless, Prahalad's analysis and Grameen's early successes at least indicate ways in which the wealth gap could be closed.

Which raises the question: What effects will this richer/poorer trend bring for your particular industry and company?

TREND 3. THE FUTURE OF GLOBALIZATION AND THE MYTH OF A SINGLE MARKET

Accelerated globalization will have impacts and consequences on all organizations and therefore must be an input into the leaders' strategic thinking and planning. Decisions affecting product design, manufacturing sites, marketing approaches, distribution systems, and customer service will vary greatly from one market to another. The reason is simple. Although the marketplace will be global in scope, it is not now, nor will it be, homogeneous in character. In Europe, language and culture differ in each country. Customs and traditions vary greatly from one Asian nation to the next. Yet local market strategies, while adapting to the nuances of individual markets, must also ensure that the underlying basis of the corporate strategy remains the gyroscope that keeps the various units in sync.

The CEO of Ascendas, a Decision Processes International (DPI) client based in Singapore and the leading provider of business space in Asia, bears testimony to this reality. Chong Siak Ching states it this way: "Because we run an international organization, it is critical that the HQ organization and country-level management are part of the development of the corporate strategy. They own it and can ensure alignment to it." The key word here is *alignment.* Rather than push the corporate strategy down the throats of the regional management, Ascendas went on to develop fine-tuned country-level strategies for each major Asian market.

The United States has always been a multicultural mixture. In the last 30 years or so, Hispanic, Korean, Japanese, Filipino, and Vietnamese immigrants—to name but a few groups—have continued to change the fabric of the country. Companies operating in an environment like this will often need to adapt local market strategies even within one such country. An example is American food companies that create market approaches specifically tailored to emerging Hispanic and Asian communities.

Those operating in these widely varied and changing markets will need to decide how, and to what extent, their approaches will need to be customized to accommodate these local differences. Like Ascendas, they need to answer the question: "How do we bring together and optimize the benefits of global and local trends?"

To "Think Global, Act Local" will be a fundamental rule of success in the future for international business. 3M, one of Decision Processes International's long-term clients, has been a rare exception to the common failure of companies to adapt to local circumstances. At 3M the notion of "Think Global, Act Local" is part and parcel of their operating culture. Companies will have to act locally, in a marketing and selling sense, in order to flush out the distinctive needs of each market. But they will have to think globally on a manufacturing, distribution, and customer service basis in order to achieve the required levels of critical mass for costs and value.

Long ago Sir John Harvey-Jones, the former chair of Imperial Chemical Industries (ICI), explained the phenomenon well at a meeting of the American Chamber of Commerce in London: "The cliché that the world is a single market is, in reality, not true. Each market requires different responses, and it is the ability to read that response and apply that response which will be the key." This will require companies to be global in perspective but culturally sensitive on a market-to-market basis.

Gary DiCamillo, when he was CEO of Black & Decker, explained how his company coped with this phenomenon: "As you go around the world, many power tools are used in similar ways so that there need not be major differences in the products. We don't need to reinvent the power tool in every country, but rather, we have a common product and adapt it to individual markets. The products are marketed quite differently in some cases due to local customs."

The need for executives to become global strategists, able to work as deftly in Beijing as in Toledo or Cape Town, will accelerate exponentially. Businesses will have to learn global strategies and tactics in order to compete successfully. In the light of global expansion, leaders will need to compete with new international rivals, many of whom play to a different set of rules.

For example, SABMiller has become the second largest global brewer, with more than 200 beer brands and some 70,000 employees in over 75 countries. They are also one of the world's largest bottlers of Coca-Cola products. For 50 years, as a South African–based company, they were confined to the South African market by international sanctions. After the miraculous change to democracy in South Africa, the sanctions were lifted, and immediately, using the skills honed in the South African market, they embarked on a major international acquisition strategy.

As SABMiller's own history document states: "We've become a global leader by excelling locally—nurturing strong, local brands and building brand portfolios that meet the needs of consumers in each of our markets. Our portfolio of brands includes premium international beers such as Pilsner Urquell, Peroni Nastro Azzurro, Miller Genuine Draft, and Grolsch, as well as leading local brands such as Aguila, Castle, Miller Lite, and Tyskie."

Theirs is a phenomenal success story based on the principle of "Think Global, Act Local." It shows what is possible when leaders are equipped with the ability to navigate unfamiliar terrain. Corporate management teams will require finely tuned competitive skills to prosper against such global foes in the future.

Which raises the question: How will you and other leaders within your organization craft agile strategies and business models that are built around a central core yet are reflective of local strategic variables?

TREND 4. THE FUTURE OF DIFFERENTIATED KNOWLEDGE

We couldn't put it better ourselves than Thomas Friedman, the Pulitzer Prize—winning author of *The World Is Flat*, in which he said: "As information is shared globally and insight is commoditized, the best returns go to those who can produce nonstandard, differentiated knowledge." This is the essence of innovation and can be generated only by finely tuned critical thinking skills that enhance the ability of managers to synthesize information—many leaders may stare at the same set of facts but not all are equipped to draw "winning" conclusions.

Friedman has made a convincing case that quicker and easier knowledge sharing has flattened the world. Through his multiple examples from India and China, in particular, he has highlighted how the alignment of increasing globalization, high-speed Internet connections, and new business models have all helped the likes of Infosys, Wipro, and Tata to become knowledge engines.

He makes the point that the steady transfer of know-how from the developed to the developing world has given rise to a greater need for innovation than has ever before existed in industrialized history.

Which raises the question: How will you harness the insights of leaders within your organization and channel these insights toward greater degrees of innovation?

TREND 5. THE INNOVATION RACE

3M has a standard by which it measures the performance of all its business units. Twenty-five percent of each unit's sales must come from products that did not exist five years before. This criterion has caused 3M to introduce some 200 new products each year and has given it a reputation as one of America's most innovative companies. Unfortunately, the same cannot be said for many companies in the United States. In general, U.S. companies are losing their innovative edge.

Many of these firms' market losses can be attributed to a lack of emphasis on product and process innovations. *Product innovations* create new market opportunities, and in many industries are the catalyst behind growth and profitability. *Process innovations*, on the other hand, enable firms to produce existing products more efficiently. As such, process innovations are among the main determinants of productivity growth. In this technologically dynamic era, without a continual stream of product *and* process innovations, firms soon lose their ability to compete effectively.

The rise and continued evolution of "quantitative" management systems and the short-term, risk-avoidance mentality that they engender has been attributed to the declining competitiveness in the United States in particular. As a result of risk avoidance, it has been shown that the United States has often lost out to Japan on the commercialization of technologies it created. For example, Ampex created the videocassette, but Sony and JVC exploited the technology. Sony also saw the potential of the Bell Laboratories transistor. The recently bankrupt Kodak invented digital imaging, a sector now dominated by the likes of Canon and Nikon of Japan. The *New York Times* writer Adam Davidson recently speculated that the next wave of commercialization would not come from Japan but rather from China.

There is good reason for this. Not only does the Chinese government—and other Asian governments for that matter—have the resources to pump into R&D, the very structure of their "version" of capitalism promotes a longer-term view. The state-controlled and/or family-owned firms in Asia and beyond don't have to play to the rules of the latest quantitative game in town or pander to the needs of short-term shareholders and analysts.

Which raises the question: How will innovation change competitive behavior in your particular industry?

TREND 6. THE INFORMATION EXPLOSION

"Data, data everywhere. . . . Information has gone from scarce to superabundant. That brings huge new benefits, but also big headaches," says Kenneth Cukier in a recent article in the *Economist:*

> When the Sloan Digital Sky Survey started work in 2000, its telescope in New Mexico collected more data in its first few weeks than had been amassed in the entire history of astronomy. Now, a decade later, its archive contains a whopping 140 terabytes of information. A successor, the Large Synoptic Survey Telescope, due to come on stream in Chile in 2016, will acquire that quantity of data *every five days*.
>
> Such astronomical amounts of information can be found closer to Earth too. Walmart, the retail giant, handles more than 1 million customer transactions every hour, feeding databases estimated at more than 2.5 petabytes—the equivalent of 167 times the books in America's Library of Congress. Facebook, the social networking website, is home to 40 billion photos. And decoding the human genome involves analyzing 3 billion base pairs—which took 10 years the first time it was done in 2003 but can now be achieved in one week.

So what are the implications of this information explosion? There is no doubt that *more accurate* information contributes to better decision making. It is also true that *too much information* can paralyze decision making. Waiting for more, or perfect, information can delay a decision and cause the decision maker to "miss the boat." In this decade, people will require more acute skills and thinking processes to be able to separate relevant from irrelevant information more quickly and thus make better and timelier decisions. There will also be less room for error since most wrong decisions will have greater and more far-reaching negative consequences. A minor decision gone wrong may have repercussions around the globe.

In his recent article "Welcome to the Information Age—174 Newspapers a Day," Richard Alleyne, science correspondent for the *Daily Telegraph*, wrote:

> If you think that you are suffering from information overload, then you may be right. A new study shows everyone is bombarded by the equivalent of 174 newspapers of data a day. The growth in the Internet, 24-hour television, and mobile phones means that we now receive five times as much information every day as we did in 1986. But that pales into insignificance compared with the growth in the amount of information we churn out through e-mail, Twitter, social networking sites, and text messages. Every day the average person produces six newspapers worth of information compared with just two and a half pages 24 years ago—nearly a 200-fold increase.

Leaders around the globe will need to update their "cognitive firmware" to cope.

Social media such as Twitter will not only continue the acceleration of the information explosion but also put pressure on organizations to both share and respond to information in real time. Recently the usually hyperefficient subway system in Singapore suffered two major failures within a week. When criticized over its handling of the cases, in particular its lack of communication, Singapore Mass Rapid Transit provoked ire and laughter in equal measure when in response it created a Twitter account that operated from 9 a.m. to 6 p.m. only! Twitter is a global phenomenon. The South African Press Association (SAPA) recently reported that South Africa tweets the most on the African continent with more than 5 million messages sent in the last three months of 2011. According to research by Portland

Communications and Tweetminster, more than 11.5 million geo-located tweets originating on the continent and a survey of 500 of Africa's most active tweeters showed that the next most active country was Kenya (2,476,800). This was followed by Nigeria (1,646,212), Egypt (1,214,062), and Morocco (745,620).

Which raises the question: What are the implications of the information explosion and real-time communications in your company and industry, and how best can you use this universe of information to your advantage?

TREND 7. THE FUTURE OF ENERGY

As defined by Future Agenda, one of the implications of the aforementioned "certainty" key resource constraints is its impact on energy, and in particular, our overdependency on fossil fuels.

The Future Agenda report states:

> [With] the increasing global susceptibility to the impacts of climate change, momentum for change is building. However, we are not yet at a stage where either global agreement will take effect or where technological breakthroughs will provide new solutions; nor are there credible alternative pathways on the table for developing economies.

Despite the lack of global consensus on climate change, legislation is fast being introduced in local jurisdictions, driving a need for companies to accept the reality and adopt programs that if properly conceived and implemented can deliver real benefits to their businesses. The most impactful will be programs where the revenue benefits will substantially exceed the costs, with the overwhelming benefit of preserving our beautiful world for the future.

In a recent article titled "Why should CEOs care about climate change? Is it a nuisance or growth opportunity?" Muriel Chinoda, senior associate, DPI Africa and a noted expert in climate change, ponders the strategic risk and opportunities arising from this controversial topic. She elaborates:

> Whatever your views on climate change's causes and possible dangers, strategic pressures are being created by rising environmental concerns and threats of the pledges, commitments, laws, and regulations being enacted around the world to curb greenhouse gas emissions, as well as increasing demands by consumers. Climate change has become an unavoidable input into any organization's strategic process. The implications, risks, and opportunities are simply too large for a CEO to ignore.

That's why many CEOs are no longer looking at the topic as an operational headache to be managed but as a strategic opportunity to be exploited.

Which raises the question: What implications will climate change and energy constraints have in your particular industry and company?

TREND 8. THE FUTURE OF HUMAN HEALTH

The tiny state of Singapore—unlike Great Britain, its former colonial ruler, which seems to view health costs as an economic millstone—is one of many countries that has bet significant sums on human health as a major driver of economic growth. The Singapore government has invested hundreds of millions of dollars to establish a dedicated, built-from-scratch biomedical research community, known as Biopolis, and it has enticed the best and the brightest researchers and research organizations in the field to the country. Due to its renowned efficiency and highly developed health sector, Singapore is also a major beneficiary of "medical tourism" in Asia.

Future Agenda agrees that healthcare presents major new opportunities for innovation: "The world of health and nutrition is one in which there are many significant technological and social changes on the horizon. For instance, stem cell research and more detailed use of the information we have on the human genome are providing a plethora of new development opportunities."

As we move toward 2020, the generally larger, older, more overweight population, at least in developed countries, will necessitate a number of major policy decisions around food supply, health funding, and even end-of-life management. Admittedly, some of these will be more relevant to certain countries than others, yet at the same time, we must not lose sight of the fact that some health issues connect us all. Fears over new global pandemics, such as bird flu, are good examples. In response, new business models will also move rapidly around the world to make healthcare more efficient.

Which raises the question: What are the implications of changes in the healthcare arena for your particular industry and company?

TREND 9. ECONOMIC DOWNTURNS AND UNCERTAINTY

Unfortunately the mantra "History repeats itself" applies to economic trends, especially downturns. The majority of DPI clients worldwide, even those in Asia, foresee shorter and more unpredictable economic cycles. Sadly, recessions are here to stay and will probably raise their ugly heads more often.

Savvy leaders realize that every cloud has a silver lining. Rex Glanville, chair, DPI Africa, recently said, in exploring what it takes to survive and thrive in hard times:

> While the discussions on how the world may look over the next decade are interesting and valid, many CEOs' major concern right now is survival in the worst local and global economic conditions since the Great Depression. However, CEOs should consider that economic downturns are often opportunities to launch unique new products while their competitors are in retreat. What do successes

such as MTV (launched in 1981), the iPod (2001), and Google's Android (2008) all have in common? Well, for starters they were all launched in the midst of recessions.

Economic downturns, recessions, slumps—these terms send chills down the spine of even the most robust of business leaders. Whenever the economy takes a dive, in boardrooms across the world, planning gets underway for hard times ahead. There is great temptation, however, to cocoon when things get difficult—cutting back on risk and innovation, curtailing spending, downsizing, and generally pulling back, hoping to come out unscathed.

Worse still, CEOs may take the "easy" route of across-the-board cuts that ignore opportunities and regional variations and most importantly, the critical need to sustain strategic competencies. Yet it is exactly these old reflexes that kick in during an uncertain economic outlook—cutting people and programs—that have to be rethought.

"The best time for risk taking and innovation is when the economy is challenging," agrees F. Franks, president of the U.S.-based management consulting practice Franks Consulting Group. "While most businesses retrench, those that take risks and push innovation stand out among their competition."

Successful companies such as Sony, 3M, Canon, Microsoft, Johnson & Johnson, Caterpillar, and Schwab maintain their control of their turf not by introducing "me-too" products but rather by focusing their resources on the creation of new-to-the-market products and/or improved processes.

Along with great innovative products, smart companies will find the resources to step up advertising and marketing. It may be counterintuitive, but there is plenty of evidence to show that continuing to engage in marketing during an economic downturn can sustain business and provide a competitive advantage.

A classic case in point: In 1933, in the heart of the Great Depression, Procter & Gamble (P&G) took a risk that changed the company, and advertising history. Despite protests from

shareholders, P&G president Richard Deupree created compelling radio serials, sponsored by Ivory Soap. This was the
start of what became known as "soap operas." By the time 1939
rolled around, P&G was sponsoring 21 radio programs. They
doubled their radio advertising budget every two years during
the Depression. The company is today the world's number one
maker of household products.

As Harvard Business School professor John A. Quelch
recently noted: "It is well documented that brands that increase
advertising in a recession, when competitors are cutting back,
can improve market share and return on investment at lower
cost than during good economic times."

Spending needs to be carefully planned and targeted, of
course. The key is to do more with less and to do it creatively,
thoroughly examining market strategies and revising messages
if need be. Research suggests that offering reassurance, empha-
sizing value, and empowering consumers with information is
the way to go during uncertain times, as opposed to going for
aspirational, optimistic, and light-hearted messages.

This is the time to reconnect with customers and figure out
how to add value to their experience. Solidifying relationships
with customers now means that they'll remember those who
stuck with them when times get better.

"It seems that during a downturn in the economy, businesses
of all sizes are quick to put customers last," says Franks. "No!
This is the time to reevaluate what your business is doing to
delight your customers."

Along with customers, it is also critical to look after employees. Job uncertainty means weakened employee motivation,
which can have serious effects on productivity. Overhiring in good
times and quickly resorting to downsizing as a temporary fix is
a common mistake. Recognizing the warning signs of declining
motivation and overall morale can allow managers to respond
quickly with intervention strategies aimed at boosting declining
productivity and retaining strategically important talent.

Without a doubt, there are companies that will have to take a hard look at people-related reductions. But rather than approaching expense reduction with a broad brush—if not a blunt instrument—companies should consider the areas in which any thinning of the talent ranks could undermine their strategic strengths and render them uncompetitive when the economic climate improves.

Which raises the question: How are you avoiding a batten-down-the-hatches mode and looking ahead to take actions now to exploit new opportunities when economic conditions improve?

TREND 10. THE BATTLE FOR HUMAN CAPITAL

Many of our clients talk of a "war for talent" in their industries. Good employees have always been a scarce resource, and with the ever-increasing mobility of labor—especially highly skilled labor—HR managers face a challenging future.

Yet hiring is not the sole responsibility of the HR function. The list of "best companies to work for" frequently lists the usual suspects, such as Apple, Google, Marriott, Allianz, and Accenture. It is not a coincidence that these companies are among the world's most successful, meaning that they have excellent business strategies in place. As Mike Robert, DPI's founder, has put it: "The best employees want to work for the best companies, those with distinct game-winning strategies. After all, who would have followed Alexander the Average or Frederick the Mediocre?"

Furthermore, as the world gets "flatter," it is common to find smart people working for companies that can enable them to move to more prosperous geographic regions. For example, many Indian workers in the IT sector see ASEAN as a stepping stone to Silicon Valley. How long until they step to China instead?

As the older generation retires and the younger, less experienced managers take over, there will be a critical need for organizations to teach them how to make effective decisions without the benefit of experience. Generation Y employees in developed countries need help to look at problems in a logical manner.

Which raises the question: What strategy and business model will enable you to attract, retain, and most effectively deploy the right people?

THE ONE THING THAT WON'T CHANGE!

Amid all the changes facing leaders, there is one thing that will remain constant: formulating and executing strategies and plans that will ensure survival and generate future sustainable growth and wealth for organizations have always been, and always will be, the primary and most important tasks of C-level leadership.

A vital input into this process is obtaining the best available view of what the future social, political, and economic global environment will look like in relation to the specific sandbox the organization intends to compete in. Only then can the leader be confident that plans are relevant to the anticipated conditions. Developing the best possible understanding of the various possible future playing field scenarios demands the leaders' attention so they can achieve the following:

- Protect their organizations from future threats
- Pursue future opportunities
- Attain that desired but elusive goal of sustainable organizational growth

Strategy, or indeed innovation and day-to-day operations, are not created or managed in a vacuum. They must be based on the particular environmental conditions anticipated during the period being planned for. The selected strategy has to weather the adverse environmental conditions and leverage the positive conditions to advantage. Sports provide a useful analogy. In any sport, be it baseball, cricket, soccer, or rugby, the selected game plan will inevitably consider the anticipated playing field conditions.

In a business context, therefore, the first task of the leadership team is to define the particular shape and nature of their industry's future playing field, what we at DPI call the Future Business Arena. Once this is defined, various game plans can be constructed.

This has always been an onerous task. But in a world characterized by exponentially scary levels of change in all spheres, one can well understand executive teams throwing up their hands in despair and perhaps deciding that they will pragmatically manage change as and when it occurs.

To try and manage change in this way can be fatal as long-term strategies become undermined or derailed by short-term fixes created in panic mode. Besides, at their very core no seasoned leaders, or at least the ones we work with, are comfortable with such a reactive stance. The late Steve Jobs has shown that it is possible to do more than react to change. Change, such as the ongoing ripples of the iPad in education, business, and entertainment, can be created. Yet to create change, one needs to also understand and see change and respond to the questions it raises.

THE QUESTIONS RAISED BY THE TRENDS

The trends shared above are macro, cross-industry ones, yet they raise numerous critical questions to be answered. Alas, they only scratch the surface of what a typical leader has to grapple with. By the time you've drilled down to industry- and company-level specifics, the leader can be easily overwhelmed! Deeper insight into the world of 2020 will only lead to further questions like these posed by Future Agenda:

1. How well do we recognize the big issues on the horizon?
2. How well do we understand the full implications of resource constraints?

3. Where can we use existing capabilities to create new sources of value?

4. As the world changes, what new activities will come to the fore where our skills and experience can be more effectively deployed, and how can we best take advantage of the opportunities?

5. To what extent do we expect to have influence over our human resources?

6. If the world is getting smaller and flatter and the best talent is mobile, how can we attract the key people we need for the future, how can we stimulate them, and how will we reward them?

7. Is our understanding of future areas of opportunity better than that of our peers?

8. Are we paying enough attention to what we don't know? Do we understand the future any better than others do? How vulnerable are we to change from outside, and how and where can we best understand this?

9. Are we paying enough attention to monitoring threats to both our core and potential new areas of activity? Can we create competitive advantage by spotting new opportunities earlier than others do?

10. How will we manage our reputation in the future?

11. Will we be able to communicate with stakeholders in 2020? Will we be in control of our brand, or will consumers have more influence? Are we prepared to change the way we act?

SUMMARY

What do these trends mean for corporations everywhere as they head for 2020? What will it take to answer the resultant questions?

In our view this environment will require strong leadership. It will be very good for people and organizations that develop and practice leadership skills. Proactive leadership will require the ability to detect, assess, and exploit these trends for an organization's greatest benefit. *Leadership*, however, is an elusive word that has different meanings to different people. To us, *leadership* has a very specific meaning and requires the mastery of very discrete and deliberate skills and management processes, which we will explore in the remainder of this book.

As Peter Drucker put it: "Effective leadership is not only about making speeches or being liked; leadership is defined by results, not by personal attributes." In the next chapter, we explore the notion of what leadership is in more detail.

Note: We would encourage our readers to visit the Future Agenda website for more detail: www.futureagenda.org.

CHAPTER 2

What Is Leadership?

By leadership we mean the art of getting
someone else to do something that you
want done because he wants to do it.

—DWIGHT D. EISENHOWER

Although the term *leadership* is frequently used, few executives in business today can be considered true leaders. The ultimate test of a leader is whether he or she will be followed as General Dwight Eisenhower was followed in the D-Day invasion by a task force composed of people from several different countries and cultures. For the followers to allow themselves to be led assumes their implicit belief in the leader's ability.

Discussions that take place on the subject of leadership will tend to be centered on the inspirational but less tangible "Churchillian" qualities that can inspire individuals and indeed nations to almost superhuman endeavors in pursuit of noble goals. Many will say with some justification that such leadership attributes are God-given and cannot be learned.

Many books have been written on leadership, but few have been able to describe it in comprehensible terms, nor have they been able to describe the skills of leadership in any detail except to attribute it to a "trait of personality." Good definitions defy the test of time, and Jack Welch, the former CEO of General Electric, timelessly views it this way:

> A leader is someone who can develop a vision of what he or she wants their business, their unit, their activity to do and be. Somebody who is able to articulate to the entire unit what the unit is and will gain through a sharing of the discussion—listening and talking—an acceptance of that vision. And then can relentlessly drive implementation of that vision to a successful conclusion.

Despite its age, that definition of leadership is probably as close a definition as we could conjure up ourselves. More recently, in his book *The Leadership Code,* HR guru Dave Ulrich describes leadership in terms of a five-attribute model:

- Strategist
- Executor
- Talent manager
- Human capital developer
- Personal proficiency

It is hard to fault this model. However, hidden in Welch's statement and Ulrich's model are the implicit mention of three very different sets of skills and critical thinking processes. Our view is that there are some fundamental skills of transformative leadership that can be articulated, learned, and perfected by almost anyone in any organization. *Indeed, leadership consists of mastering three critical management skills that should be practiced consciously.*

THREE FUNDAMENTAL SKILLS OF LEADERSHIP

Without mastering these three fundamental skills of leadership, the leader will not be followed. Unfortunately, none of these skills are taught in the formal education system, business schools, or any corporation's management development program. Most leaders who have acquired these skills have done so by osmosis (intuitively) or by experience on the "firing line." However, these skills can also be acquired in a conscious and deliberate manner.

The first skill is *Strategic Thinking*. It is the thought process used by a leader to formulate, articulate, and communicate a coherent vision and strategy for the organization. Followers want to know where they are being led, and those close to the leader wish to participate in the process. Beyond formulation, strategic thinking encompasses the skills of execution. A great strategy on paper is useless unless it can be put into action.

The second skill is *Innovative Thinking*. Companies need to constantly find new opportunities in order to grow. A leader must be able to initiate, promote, and develop in others these special abilities. In order to do so, he or she must understand the process of innovation and be able to instill it in every member of the organization.

The third skill is *Situation Management*, which is the ability to deal with operational problems and decisions successfully. However, operational situations must be resolved in a manner that is aligned with the strategy. Otherwise operations of the "current" business will dominate to the extent that the vision of the "new" business is forgotten. This requires a multipart process that we call *Situation Management*, comprising both rational decision making and creativity. Again, this must be part of the fabric of an organization so that issues can be addressed both incisively and decisively.

STRATEGIC THINKING

DPI's process goes beyond strategy formulation. It
unites and energizes people towards a common goal.

—FRANCIS CHAN, CEO, KAM YUEN (GROUP) INTERNATIONAL LIMITED

Strategic Thinking is the process used by a leader, and his or her leadership team, to formulate, articulate, communicate, and implement a clear, concise, and explicit strategy for the organization. Unfortunately, in many organizations the strategy of the company is not clear. It usually resides in the head of the chief executive officer exclusively and is called his or her "vision." Strategy is related to, but not to be confused with, vision. Indeed, we've never come across a CEO or unit leader who did not have a vision for his or her firm or unit.

It is the collective translation of this vision into a specific and operable *strategic profile* that is the issue. In the absence of this, other people around the CEO have to guess at the strategy. Because they have not been involved in the process, or because the CEO cannot clearly articulate the strategy, they feel no commitment to it or ownership of it. Our own experience with some 1,000 organizations of all sizes and in various industries around the world has shown that most managers are so engrossed in operational activity that they have not developed the skills to think strategically. A CEO, therefore, might wish to involve his or her team in a deliberate strategic process strictly for its educational value or because the team needs to appreciate the underlying rationale to implement the process effectively. The problem, however, is that most CEOs practice this process instinctively and are not conscious of its various steps. It is usually impossible to transfer to anyone else a skill that one cannot describe. That is why we developed the Strategic Thinking Process, which has the following broad steps.

Step 1. Assess the Environment

Any sound strategy must allow the organization to successfully deal with its environment, or, if you like, "playing field" conditions, as discussed in the previous chapter. Thus, the first step in the Strategic Thinking Process is an assessment of the qualitative variables that will be working for or against the business in the future. These variables, however, usually have been considered only at a high level by the management team and must be extracted, debated, and distilled in a structured and objective forum with an outside person facilitating the process. The qualitative variables are usually highly subjective in nature and consist of each person's view of what may or may not occur inside and, more importantly, outside the organization.

These differing views must be discussed in a rational manner in order to agree on the most important factors that the business will have to face, and they must be driven to a level of new insight that goes beyond obvious generalism.

Step 2. Determine the Business's Strategic Heartbeat

The next step is for the management team to identify which component of the business is strategically most important to the organization's survival and serves as the key determinant of the company's products, markets, and customers. In other words, which part of the business is at the root of the organization and can be leveraged by the company as its strategic weapon against its environment? This concept is known as the *Driving Force*, and it will be discussed in more detail in a subsequent chapter.

Step 3. Develop a Coherent Strategy and Business Concept

Around the key determinant, which will drive the organization forward, it is now imperative to develop a *statement of strategy* that can be communicated to the individuals who will be called on to carry it out. It needs to be articulated in terms precise and concise enough so that people can carry it around in their heads.

The statement should represent the conceptual underpinning of the organization and its raison d'être.

Over a number of years we have noticed a substantial increase in the number of corporations that attempt to construct mission or vision statements that articulate the organization's business concept. Unfortunately, most attempts to do so are fruitless because of the lack of a structured process. As a result, the leaders end up going through the motions in "visioning workshops" that yield statements that are "motherhood" in nature. Here's a good example:

> Our mission is to provide products and services of superior competitive quality and value, to achieve strong growth in sales and income, to realize consistently higher returns on equity and cash required to fuel our growth, and to have people who contribute superior performance at all levels.

This is an example of a "meaningless mission statement"—it is so general in tone and substance that everyone can agree with it. Such statements are useless as guides to help people make decisions that propel the organization in its desired direction. They contain words that sound nice and with which everyone can agree. However, when used as a filter to make decisions, they fall apart because they allow everything through. Nothing is eliminated. Over time, the statement is quietly dismissed from the psyche of the organization.

We elaborate on what it takes to craft an effective business concept in a subsequent chapter. For now, don't take our word for it. Peter Drucker, the guru of all management gurus, outlined his thesis as follows:

> Every organization, whether a business or not, has a theory of the business. Indeed, a valid theory that is clear, consistent, and focused is extraordinarily powerful. These are the assumptions that shape any organization's behavior,

dictate its decisions about what to do and what not to do, and define what the organization considers meaningful results. These assumptions are about markets. They are about identifying customers and competitors, their values and behavior. They are about technology and its dynamics, about a company's strengths and weaknesses. These assumptions are about what a company gets paid for. They are what I call a company's theory of the business.

In summary, the statement should provide clear and specific guidance to allow managers to allocate resources properly and choose the appropriate opportunities to pursue. Here are some examples of business concepts that we have helped our client organizations to construct. For reasons of confidentiality, the names of the companies involved have been omitted.

Example 1

Our strategy is to market, manufacture, and distribute saw blade products, made from strip metal stock, that provide exceptional value.

We will concentrate on high performance, material separation applications where we can leverage our integrated manufacturing capabilities to develop customized, innovative, consumable products with demonstrable advantages that bring premium prices.

We will seek out customer segments and geographic markets where the combination of superior distribution and technical support services will give us an additional competitive advantage.

Example 2

Our strategy is to provide reinsurance products to assist organizations in managing life, health, and annuity risks.

We will differentiate ourselves by leveraging our mortality and morbidity risk management expertise.

We will concentrate on market segments where we can establish and maintain a leadership position.

We will concentrate in growth-oriented, "free" geographic areas with reliable databases and predictable risk patterns where we can achieve critical mass and a balanced portfolio.

Exotic? Definitely not. Sexy? Absolutely not. Powerful? You bet!

Step 4. Paint a Full Strategic Profile

The next step is to take the concept and build upon it to paint a full picture of what the business will look like sometime in the future. This profile should be a description of the products, customers, market segments, and geographic markets that the organization will emphasize and deemphasize in the future. This profile then serves everyone as a *test bed* for the allocation of resources and the types of opportunities that are to be pursued in the future.

Step 5. Anticipate the Implications of Your Strategy

Frequently a good strategy can go astray because management did not think through its implications. The next step, then, is to test the strategy in a variety of ways to flush out its implications and identify the critical issues that will need to be addressed in order to make the strategy work. Too often these implications are not considered, and management finds itself reacting to them after the fact, instead of having anticipated them in advance and dealing with them proactively. These critical issues can then be assigned to specific people who have the responsibility to manage them to a successful resolution.

With the future "look" of the organization fully but succinctly described, and with the critical issues accurately identified, the process of implementing the strategy becomes relatively straightforward. Monitoring the progress being made on issues and drawing these issues to a conclusion will ensure the success of the strategy.

INNOVATIVE THINKING

The second fundamental skill of leadership is the ability to innovate and, in particular, to promote this kind of thinking in others. Generating concepts for new and better products, new customers, and new markets, and also for ways to improve the way in which the business is run, is key to an organization's survival. The best companies today appear driven to continuously innovate. Some organizations, however, have shown more skill at it than others. In our view, it is because these organizations have mastered the process of innovation. The key trait of leaders is to master this skill themselves and to aid subordinates in its gestation.

When we first started to look into the subject of innovation by going to our clients and observing them trying to innovate, we seemed to be entering a world of sorcery. When we asked innovative people what they or their organization felt was the origin of their skill, they gave answers such as "accidents," "flashes of genius," or "lightning bolts out of the blue." However, when we watched these people while they worked, we found no accidents. Instead, what we observed was the practice of a very systematic, deliberate, and discrete process at work, being used intuitively, but nevertheless being used. This process, which we have codified as the *Process of Innovation*, has four steps.

Step 1. Search the Environment for Opportunities

The most fundamental concept of innovation is that change is the raw material and fuel of innovation. There can be no innovation without change. Change creates turmoil, and out of turmoil comes opportunity. The more change, the more opportunity; the less change, the less opportunity.

Therefore, innovative people and organizations see change as healthy and as a consistent source of opportunity. The best innovators, however, do not wait for change to find them. They seem to know exactly where, in the environment, to search for changes that can be transformed into good business opportunities. We have identified 10 such environmental sources that will be explored in more detail in the following chapters.

Step 2. Assess and Rank the Opportunities

Not all opportunities should be pursued. There are bad, good, and excellent opportunities. Therefore, the opportunities that are found need to be ranked in terms of their potential benefit to the organization. There are four important criteria to consider in this step, which will be discussed later. From this assessment, the best opportunities, like cream, will start rising to the top of the list.

Step 3. Develop the Critical Factors for Success or Failure

The fact that an opportunity ends up at the top of the list is no guarantee that it can be pursued successfully. The third step of innovation, then, is to identify the potential best-case and worst-case outcomes that each opportunity could bring to the organization. This is important for two reasons. Firstly, we can now discuss the risk/reward relationship of each opportunity and further reduce our list to the crème de la crème of the opportunities available. Secondly, we can now identify the critical factors that will cause the best-case or worst-case scenarios to occur.

Step 4. Construct a Plan to Pursue the Best Opportunities

Some people think that good innovators are not good implementers. This is not necessarily the case. The best innovators we saw could conceptualize as well as implement their innovations successfully. They did this by anticipating actions that could prevent the negative critical factors from happening and bringing about the worst-case outcomes and by anticipating actions to promote the critical factors that would bring about the best-case scenario. These actions would then be made part and parcel of a step-by-step implementation plan to carry out each opportunity. Each step would be assigned to an "owner" for execution, together with target dates for completion and review dates to monitor progress.

Another timeless statement came from Henry Adams in 1907: "Chaos often breeds life, when order breeds habit." Although the environment and changes seem to behave in a chaotic manner, a systematic process of innovation can breed a habit that can help people and leaders deal with chaos successfully.

SITUATION MANAGEMENT

While a leader is thinking strategically in order to best position his or her organization in relation to its environment and is encouraging innovation to identify new opportunities, he or she must also deal effectively with the operational issues that surface each day and make sure the entire organization is geared up to do likewise. It is tempting to manage this through "best practices" and "standard operating procedures."

Unfortunately, this has the adverse effect of removing the ability of others to think critically. Unanticipated situations will inevitably occur. What is one to do when the operating procedure doesn't cover the oddball customer request or the unforeseen problem! Fueled by mobile phones—which make it easy to contact "the boss" rather than take responsibility—an undesired tendency is to upwardly delegate the issue through the management ranks, which slows down the resolution process, allows things to escalate for no good reason, and takes up management time on unnecessary matters.

A better approach is to equip people, including management, with the ability to critically think through unexpected situations. We call this *Situation Management*, and it is actually very viable due to this simple fact: although people seem to be bombarded by a variety of different issues from the time they arrive at work until the time they leave, there are only three types of issues that people face each day, and these issues occur over and over again. The three types of situations are *problems*, *decisions*, and *plans to be implemented*. Each of these can be resolved through the application of the critical thinking processes contained within the Situation Management framework.

The first critical thinking process is *Problem Analysis*. This process is used when we are faced with a situation in which something has gone wrong and no one knows what caused such an event to occur. Problem Analysis is a process used to logically diagnose a problem in order to identify its root cause and bring about corrective action.

Decision Analysis, on the other hand, is a process used when we are faced with having to make a choice among several options or alternatives, all of which seem to be good, and when the best alternative is not evident. Decision Analysis can help us methodically sort our way through the alternatives in order to identify the best one.

Once a tentative decision has been made, however, it must be implemented successfully, and thus the third process, *Potential Problem Analysis*, comes into play. A detailed implementation plan is drawn up and then explored for potential problems. By anticipating what might go wrong with the plan, we can also anticipate actions to prevent these potential problems from happening or, at least, have contingent actions ready to minimize their effect should they occur. The original plan is then modified to include the best preventive and contingent actions we have generated, and the modified plan is the one we pursue since it has a better chance of working than the original one.

In among all of these processes is the need on occasion to exercise creativity, for example, to develop new hypotheses for intractable problems or generate new alternatives when seemingly viable options in a decision situation cannot pass muster. The *creative process* is a pathway of steps that overcome barriers to creativity and drive new ideas to implementation.

SUMMARY

These three processes—Strategic Thinking, Innovative Thinking, and Situation Management—are the fundamental processes that transformative leaders must master in order to demonstrate true leadership qualities. They must also be able to instill these skills in their followers. Arising from the investigative work commenced by our founder, Michel Robert, in the late 1970s, DPI has codified these processes into repeatable business practices that can be learned and used by groups to arrive at mutual conclusions, agreement, alignment, and successful deployment.

- The *Strategic Thinking Process* provides leaders with the tool to articulate their vision and involve their team in the process so that team members understand and buy into the process, thereby motivating them to adopt it as their own. Usually people can more easily implement something that they understand and for which they feel a real sense of ownership, which results from participating in the process.
- The *Process of Innovation* provides leaders with a tool to promote the notion of continuous improvement, which has always been a must for any organization. In this increasingly competitive world, innovation has become vital for survival. Our process demystifies innovation and puts it into terms that make it a repeatable business practice.
- The processes that make up *Situation Management* are key skills to master in order to deal effectively with the day-to-day issues that arise. While some of these issues can be operational in nature, we cannot go forward without dealing with today's concerns, crises, problems, and decisions.

The next sections of this book cover each of the above processes in turn.

We have created these processes to enable leaders to pass on, or teach, these skills to others. We cannot do this until we are fully conscious of the processes or methods we use to achieve success. Good athletes usually do not make good coaches because, while they were athletes, they never analyzed the process or method that they were practicing and that made them successful. As a result, when they become coaches, they are unable to describe and impart these skills. The best coaches, on the other hand, were not necessarily the best athletes but were, rather, "students of the game." These are the people who studied the methods or processes used by successful athletes; they discovered them and now can pass them on to others. A casual jogger does not necessarily pay much attention to the mechanics of jogging. However, if the jogger wishes to compete successfully in a marathon, he or she needs to become familiar with the technique, or process, of running in order to run in the most effective manner.

The same is true of leadership. The thinking processes essential to leadership can be studied and learned. We have studied leaders in many organizations, and the processes described briefly above are the ones that these people had mastered.

A good leader will need to develop the conscious use of these processes in his or her team in order to lead effectively. The reason is simple: it is a lot easier to lead a well-trained army than a bunch of ragamuffins. During peacetime, an army needs few leaders, but during a time of war, it needs many. The same is true during a time of commercial warfare. The more leaders you have in your organization, the higher the probability of winning. To generate more leaders, every existing leader needs to be a coach, a topic we explore in Chapter 13.

Once the processes are codified and articulated, the leader, with the help of these trained facilitators, then can institutionalize them into repeatable business practices. In other words, over time these processes can become reflexive. The notion of cascading these processes down the organization is critical to the success of a leader. Why so? Unlike what many think, a leader in business is not only a leader of people but also a manager of processes. The processes that the leader puts into place in the organization will lead people to behave in a certain manner.

The infusion of these three fundamental processes throughout the organization becomes fundamental to an organization's culture and forms the basis for ongoing success. We discuss this topic in Chapter 14.

There is a school of thought that holds that only well-resourced organizations with deep pockets are significantly advantaged to prevail in the competitive arena. That has not been true in our experience. Rather, regardless of size and resources, we have consistently found that *winning organizations are characterized by their consistent ability to out-think rather than out-muscle their opponents.* To do so, the first critical thinking skill they must master is to think strategically, the topic of the next chapter.

PART 2

THE LEADER AS STRATEGIST

CHAPTER 3

Obstacles to Transformative Strategic Thinking

f the realm of the transformative leader is to enable the organization to out-think, not out-muscle, the competition, how do you do that? How do you as the leader develop a winning strategy? How can you learn this skill? And how can you bring other key people into the process so that they understand, buy into, and own it?

RETHINKING THE ORGANIZATION'S STRATEGY

As the captain of an organization in your industry, there are a number of reasons why you may feel it is time for you to rethink your organization's strategy and forge a winning strategy that will cause your organization to *survive and thrive in times of change*. In many cases the *strategy review* is linked purely to

43

the annual budgeting ritual. A familiar statement heard around the boardrooms of organizations globally is, "We need to complete our budgets for next year, so we will be planning our strategy breakaway." We find many organizations get into this mode because they "have to" rather than considering the more important question: "Are there internal or external factors that indicate that we *need* to review our strategy?"

Our engagements with clients across the world have shown that transformative leaders think beyond the annual planning ritual and proactively look to address key issues impacting their organization and its position in the marketplace. They respond to key strategic stimuli as and when they occur, regardless of the timing of the "corporate planning cycle." Some have realized that the internal planning processes or methodologies they engage in every year are not delivering the sort of results they are expecting. They may be simply "going through the motions" and therefore unable to craft the future strategy they know in their hearts is possible. Signs highlighting the need for robust strategic thinking can take many forms and arrive at any time. Many times they take the form of the following. The organization may:

- Be at a crossroads in the industry and must decide on a new direction
- Have execution issues because there is not total buy-in at the executive management or even senior management level
- Simply not be growing fast enough
- Have a "new CEO" who needs to "make his or her mark" and "get up to speed" in unison
- Face a very dynamic business environment with a potential knockout punch on the horizon

Dr. Stephen Lee, then the newly appointed CEO at Lee Kum Kee Holdings, fell into one of these categories: "As the new CEO from a different industry, I was gratified that the DPI

Strategic Thinking Process has helped me and my executive team to formulate a cutting-edge strategy in just two months."

Whatever the reason, these organizations and their leaders realize that the future rests in their hands and that it is the ability of the entire team to think critically and strategically that will determine success or failure. Most also realize that such skills are not readily available in-house. All organizations have a strategic planning process, yet few that we know had a formal process of strategic thinking before we arrived on the scene. The process we describe in this and the next chapter is a proven way to elevate your collective thinking to the next level. With appropriate facilitation it can rigorously interrogate and challenge the "way things are done" to develop this winning strategy.

Martin Banner, CEO of National Airways Corporation in South Africa, told us:

> When I came in, the management had been going away each year on a strategic planning conference, but I wanted to find a methodology that would offer more structure to that process. I interviewed several companies, and DPI was the company of choice. What I liked about the DPI process was that I thought people would grasp it easily. It would walk us through a series of steps, challenging us on every aspect of the business. And within a three-day period, we would come out with a very meaningful conclusion. And that's exactly what happened.

OBSTACLES THAT GET IN THE WAY OF SUPREMACY

There are several strategic obstacles that leaders encounter when they are trying to develop and deploy a *game changing* strategy. Among these are that leaders may:

- Confuse strategy with vision
- Assume all agree on what a strategy is
- Be developing a strategy for today's market, not the future playing field
- Be developing a strategy for adequacy, not supremacy
- Think only about conventional competition, not possible disrupters
- Assume that the team will be "on board"
- Perceive lack of execution as an execution, not formulation, issue
- Fail to adequately resource the execution effort

OBSTACLE 1. CONFUSING STRATEGY WITH VISION

The first obstacle in developing a game changing strategy is confusing strategy with vision. All CEOs that we work with have a "vision" in their heads as to what they want their company to "look like" at some time in the future. Frequently, that "look" is different from what the company "looks like" today. They employ and deploy the assets and resources of their organization in pursuit of that future vision. (See Figure 3.1.)

The Purposes of a Vision

A vision serves several purposes in an organization. First and foremost, it captures the organization's *future intent*. A vision should stand the test of time and perpetuate the enterprise over long time frames. A vision can serve several purposes:

- *A vision bonds.* A vision can give people, possessing a diverse set of skills, languages, personalities, and cultures, a common cause, and it can direct their energies toward a unifying goal.
- *A vision inspires.* Although all corporations measure their progress over time with numbers—growth, profits, or both—numbers generally do not inspire ordinary people to do extraordinary things. But a more noble vision and strategy can inspire beyond anyone's expectation.

FIGURE 3.1 **FUTURE VISION**

- *A vision is an anchor.* When times are difficult, a vision gives an organization an anchor that will steady the ship and hold everyone together until the storm passes.
- *A vision is a potent competitive tool.* Having a sense of what one wants to become when grown up gives the organization an enormous competitive advantage.

Vision is a critically important concept for any transformative leader. The impact of not having a clear vision or believing he didn't need one was experienced by Lou Gerstner after mouthing the words "IBM doesn't need a vision or strategy" at his first press conference the week after being named CEO.

When he returned to his office after the press conference, he was immediately bombarded by an avalanche of phone calls. But this onslaught of calls didn't come from the press or other outsiders. The calls came from his own employees who wanted to remind him that Thomas Watson had made IBM one of the world's most successful companies through his "vision" of automating data processing with computers that would "substantially increase the productivity of corporations and contribute to raising the standard of living of people all over the world."

Despite its importance, vision is not to be confused with strategy. The purpose of vision is to mobilize a large population of people, who might not have any other attachment to an organization than that it is their job and source of income. It must have certain attributes in order to get ordinary people to do extraordinary things:

- *A vision must be clear.* The vision cannot be ambiguous. Most people in an organization do not want to be leaders—they simply want to be good followers. As such, what they want to know from their leaders is this: "Where are you taking me so I can decide whether I want to follow you there?" As a result, the leader must design a clear vision that can quickly and clearly be understood by all employees.
- *A vision must be compelling.* A goal of becoming a billion-dollar company will not motivate ordinary people to do extraordinary things. Numbers usually are not compelling enough to mobilize large groups of people to want to achieve beyond their capabilities. In order to motivate people to overachieve, the vision must "compel" people to want to overachieve voluntarily. Thus the reason that Steve Jobs attracted John Scully to join Apple, even though Scully had a very lucrative job with Pepsi—it was not the promise of large financial incentives but rather the "opportunity to change the world." What foresight Steve Jobs exhibited back in 1971! That is exactly what the PC industry, led in large part by Jobs and Apple, has done.
- *A vision must be distinctive.* Not many people want to work for an imitator, where every transaction the company engages in turns out to be based strictly on price. That is not a fun

world. The best companies have a *distinctive* vision that does not attempt to imitate their competitors but sets them apart from those competitors. Like the Triple Crown champion racehorse Secretariat, their notion of competition is not to run side-by-side with their competitors but rather to lead the next best competitor by 31 lengths, pulling farther and farther ahead with each lap of the business cycle. As Samuel Johnson once said, "No man has achieved greatness by imitating another man."

- *A vision must be consistent.* A vision that is constantly being adjusted is usually not going to impress anyone, particularly your own troops. Visions that are forever changing reflect the lack of any forward thinking and will become the butt of everyone's corporate jokes—the proverbial "vision of the week."

The Vision-Strategy Relationship

Although the concepts of vision and strategy are frequently used, few executives understand the relationship between them. Let us attempt to demystify these two separate but complementary concepts. *Vision*, in our view, is the construction of a mental picture of what an organization should look like sometime in the future. A vision is usually long term in nature, typically decades and in some instances centuries! *Strategy*, in our view, is the process of leaders' converting that future picture into a tangible *future strategic profile* that they then use as their filter for decision making in order to grow the company over a specific time frame. Strategy comprises a verbal description of the *business concept* and other details that provide a clear and explicit "picture" of the next destination of the organization in pursuit of the vision. It also describes how the enterprise will deploy resources to realize that future strategic profile.

For example, Ascendas, a DPI client, has the vision of being the leading provider of business space in Asia. The strategy, or business concept, that drills down into what the vision specifically means is as follows:

Ascendas' strategy is to provide **total integrated solutions** to our customers that extend beyond business space.

1. Integrated communities. We will create and manage distinctive spaces that inspire innovation and excellence in our customers and users within a secure and sustainable Ascendas integrated community, comprising mixed-use developments anchored by business space.
2. Integrated customer solutions. We will create integrated solutions as a business partner to help our customers grow their business and succeed in our space.

DPI client Hennie Du Plessis, the former CEO of Bytes Healthcare Solutions (BHS) in South Africa, agrees that that vision then needs to be forged into a clear strategy:

This unique approach intrigued the BHS team in part because it would enable the company's management to forge their own strategy from the vision we had of the future and by debating all the relevant issues with the assistance of a skilled facilitator. From this we obtained a strategy that was well understood and agreed upon. Further, and perhaps more importantly, we got a clear action plan with responsibilities, timelines for completion, and a management process to keep the implementation on track.

OBSTACLE 2. ASSUMING THAT ALL AGREE ON WHAT A STRATEGY IS

The second obstacle leaders encounter when trying to develop a game changing strategy is that they cannot agree on what a strategy is. Each executive has his or her own view or definition of what a *strategy* is. This is not surprising. Even the strategy gurus that confused leaders turn to when seeking an answer cannot agree!

The Strategy-Operations Relationship

Since the mid-1970s many books have been published on the subject of strategy. Unfortunately, most of these books have confused rather than demystified this subject. The reason, in our view, is that each author uses the word *strategy* with a different meaning. Some authors define *strategy* as the goal or objective, while others define it as the means or the tactics. Others view strategy as long-term planning versus short-term. After reading most of these books, we became as confused as their authors.

Defining *Strategy* and *Operations*

Our definitions are simple. *Strategy* is what, and *operations* is how. *Strategy* determines what you want to become as a company, and *operations* determines how you get there.

Strategy and *operations* require different processes of thinking and contain different concepts. Our experience has shown that few companies are highly proficient at both. In fact, all organizations can be found in one of four modes of proficiency around these two skills, which are illustrated by the matrix shown in Figure 3.2.

Some organizations are proficient at both strategy and operations. In other words, they have a clear strategy that is sound and well understood (what), and they are very competent operationally (how). (See Figure 3.3.)

Some organizations belong in another quadrant—strategically competent (what) but operationally ineffective (how). (See Figure 3.4.)

In even another quadrant we find the worst of both worlds—companies that have shown incompetence at both (what and how). (See Figure 3.5.)

FIGURE 3.2 STRATEGY VS. OPERATIONS

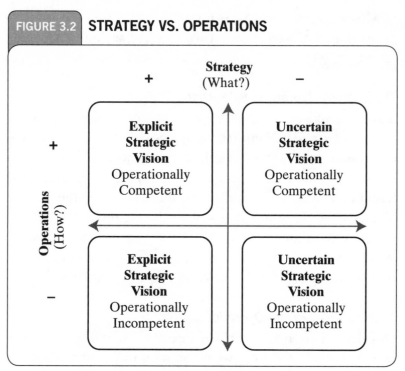

FIGURE 3.3 QUADRANT A

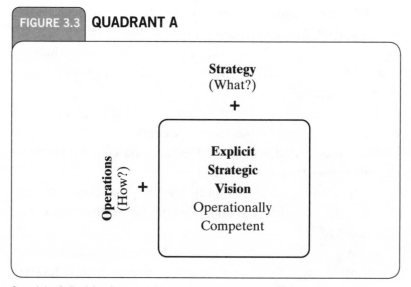

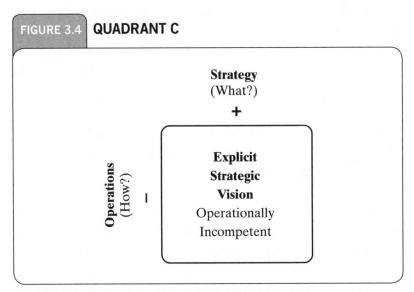

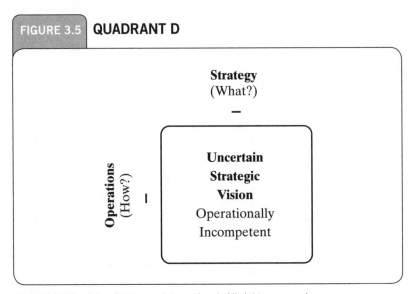

The quadrant in which we find most companies however, is the upper right—operationally competent but strategically deficient. (See Figure 3.6.)

These companies belong to the Christopher Columbus School of Management:

- When he left, he did not know where he was going.
- When he got there, he did not know where he was.
- When he got back, he could not tell where he had been.

When his company used the DPI Strategic Thinking Process, Robert Evans, turnaround specialist and former CEO of Material Sciences Corporation, noted that the DPI process emphasized thinking versus planning: "Some consultants actually develop a plan, deliver it to you, and tell you that's the plan you ought to execute. DPI doesn't do that. The company provided a thinking process that enabled us to create the strategy ourselves."

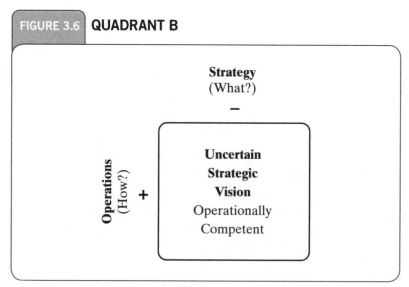

FIGURE 3.6 QUADRANT B

Strategy
(What?)

−

Operations
(How?)

+

Uncertain
Strategic
Vision
Operationally
Competent

Now looking at the four quadrants again in Figure 3.7, in which quadrant would you place your organization?

If you chose the top right quadrant, you have placed yourself with 80 percent of the firms with whom we work, and you can consider yourself normal. The reason for this is that most firms are so involved in operational activity that they do not spend enough time thinking about the future of the business.

This view was supported by Gary Holland, president and CEO of DataCard Corporation from 1982 to 1992. He commented:

> In the first two to three hours of the meeting with DPI,
> I was astonished that our senior management group
> had no concept of our strategy, and disagreed with
> it once they learned of it! I was happy about DPI's

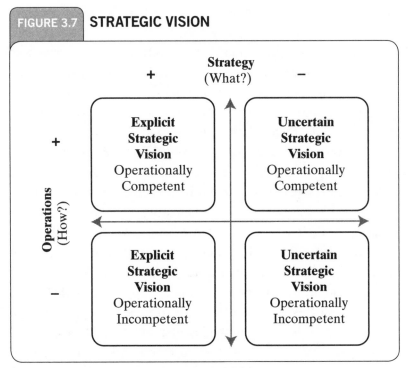

FIGURE 3.7 **STRATEGIC VISION**

intervention because, at the conclusion, we all knew and agreed with our strategy. There was absolutely no question about our beliefs and direction.

OBSTACLE 3. STRATEGIZING FOR TODAY, NOT TOMORROW

The third obstacle to developing a game changing strategy arises when leaders develop a strategy for today's market and don't think about the future playing field. Globally, more and more CEOs with whom we work tell us that it is not possible to predict the future, and it is therefore impossible to create a strategy for that future because changes are occurring faster and faster.

Political and economic conditions, computer and biomedical technology, market and client needs, climate change and sustainability, to name a few factors, are changing faster and in more unexpected ways than ever before. Thus many claim, "No one can keep up with—much less predict—what else will happen in the future." This may be partly true. Yet we believe that the view that change happens too quickly to be anticipated is somewhat of a myth. Our experience leads us to a different hypothesis.

To forge a winning strategy that will cause your organization to *survive and thrive in times of change*, in our opinion, there are two ways to deal with change in your business arena. You deal with it either proactively or reactively. We have found that the vast majority of executives deal with most changes in a reactive mode. They have developed skills that are corrective in nature rather than being proactive or anticipatory. Proof of this is in the pudding. If their key skill was anticipatory, why were the CEOs and senior executives of thousands of corporations around the world caught by surprise by the advent of the Internet? Why do they get caught out by new innovations in products and services or methodologies? Why are they surprised by new breakthrough inventions like laser technologies or more recently social networking media? We believe they just weren't looking. Many of these so-called changes have been around for years.

But how can you predict the future? How can you create the crystal ball that will give you the clues as to how things will change in the future? We mentioned earlier that Professor Peter Drucker had an uncanny ability to predict the future. That ability lay in his "looking out the window and seeing things that other people did not see." But how do you do that?

Envisioning the Future

"How can anyone anticipate what the future will look like? The future is a big and confused place." This question is reasonable, yet our premise has a very simple and rational explanation. When analyzed more closely, many things that look big and complex at first glance turn out to be an assembly of a limited number of smaller elements with a limited range of variables. In reality, the *Future Business Arena* (or the "sandbox," as we at DPI refer to it) in which any organization will compete consists of 12 discrete compartments in which disruptive trends, or indications of the future, might emerge:

1. Economic and monetary areas
2. Political and regulatory areas
3. Social and demographic changes
4. Market conditions and trends
5. Customer attributes and habits
6. Competitor profiles
7. Technology evolution
8. Manufacturing capabilities and processes
9. Product design, content, and features
10. Sales and marketing methods
11. Distribution methods and systems
12. Natural, human, and financial resources

With disciplined exploration of the 12 facets within a Future Business Arena, haphazard guesswork is replaced by specific insight. This gives a leader some confidence that conclusions are not being derived entirely from speculative "crystal ball" gazing and that future conclusions are based, as far as possible, on a stable logical path. The task then becomes less intimidating, and it can be tackled with a greater degree of confidence.

Once the complexity of the Future Business Arena has been deciphered into these 12 "building blocks," one can begin to anticipate what the future will look like. By placing yourself and your key executives in a "time machine" and moving yourself ahead x years and describing the characteristics you believe each compartment will have at that time, you will have a very good picture of the future.

The good news is that you don't need a guru to predict the future. Our contention is that most changes that will impact your business 3 to 5 or even 10 years from now are in place in the Future Business Arena in some form today. Most changes that will affect a company announce themselves well in advance of the time they will strike.

Decoding the Future Today

Naturally, one cannot be 100 percent right about the future, and totally unexpected events do show up, such as the 2008 Global Financial Crisis, which caught the world by surprise. But was this event really unpredicted? As far back as 2001, cover stories in the *Economist* included these: in 2001, "Can the World Escape a Recession?"; in 2002, "Doldrums: The World Economy and How to Rescue It"; in 2004, "Scares Ahead for the World Economy"; and in 2007, "The Trouble with the Housing Market." There were many more articles that were asking questions, giving clues that a major event was manifesting itself in the future and would impact the business arena of nearly all organizations globally.

So if one knows where to look, one can decode the future today. Our thesis is that the future is not one place but rather a collection of five places:

1. The future ahead
2. The future beyond
3. The future behind
4. The future around
5. The future beside

The Future Ahead

This *future ahead* is a future that has already started but has not yet fully arrived. Like a train, it has already left the station, but it has not yet arrived at its final destination. However, its end destination can be determined. In fact, the future ahead comes on three sets of predictable "rails":

- *The future that can be projected by extrapolating current phenomena.* An example is demographics. It was predicted over four decades ago that by the year 2010, in the United States, 50 percent of the population would be over 50 years old and 30 percent would be over 60, and 1 million people would be over 100 years old. When forecast, that future had already left the station but had not yet arrived at its ultimate destination, but it will arrive. This future started after World War II, and it has been progressing through the U.S. population and building momentum each year since then. That trend could have been projected accurately for the last two or three decades because it was a trend that was traveling along an irreversible, preestablished train track.
- *The future that is branching along two or more sets of paths, or rails.* An example of the *branching future* came with the introduction of the videocassette recorder, or VCR. When that event occurred, two standards emerged in the United States— Betamax and Video Home System (VHS)—and the eventual winner was not clearly identifiable until both standards had been in the marketplace for several years. Right from the beginning, however, the advantages of VHS were clear, and

anyone could have projected that it would probably be the winning standard. Another that emerged after this was the digital video disc (DVD) versus Blu-ray recording on compact discs (CDs). The eventual winner was and is clear: Blu-ray.

Another example that has not yet played itself out might be the electric/gasoline hybrid car versus the hydrogen fuel-cell car versus the gasoline-powered car. The political and environmental problems associated with burning hydrocarbons and the need for alternatives are obvious. But what branch will the future ahead follow—and how might that and other related changes affect your business?

- *The future that is constrained because it comes with some predictable boundaries.* Examples of these are countries enacting legislation or scientists discovering new laws of physics, engineering, or chemistry or clarifying or disproving laws already in existence.

The Future Beyond

The *future beyond* is a future that is beyond the *future ahead*, and it is also a projectable future that has already started but not yet arrived. Its end destination is unpredictable or undeterminable because it has a number of end possibilities or outcomes. The important issue is that the trends be identified and put onto the radar screen of the executive team and monitored so that its direction to a potential end destination can be determined.

Examples of these issues are the ongoing changes in Europe in terms of the European Union and the single currency. If it had been stated in 1985 that these changes would occur, no one would have believed it because communism was still at the heart of Europe's operating fabric.

The Future Behind

What can one learn about the future by looking at the *future behind*? The answer is: history repeats itself. The future behind is one that happened in the past, yet it provides a template for the interpretation of current events that will have future impli-cations. Looking at the future behind can give us great insights about the future ahead. What changes or trends that are hap-pening in your sandbox today might have blueprints in the past to help you to see where they might be going?

Andrew Grove, the former CEO of Intel, once said: "If you want to know what will happen in technology in the next 10 years, simply look at what has happened in the last 10 years."

The Future Around

The *future around* is a future that is already present in your sandbox but is not yet fully deployed. These are events or trends that are in your sandbox and will amplify over time. If you have not taken stock of these events, they will catch you by surprise and bite you badly.

An example is the work going on in the area of human genomes. No pharmaceutical company in the world can afford to ignore the developments occurring in this area of its sandbox because these discoveries will dramatically change the nature of the company's future products. Another similar area of devel-opment is bioelectronics—the convergence of biological and electronic and even mechanical technologies. Might an exercise equipment company be interested in that?

The Future Beside

The fifth type of future you will encounter consists of events or trends already in place in adjacent sandboxes that will eventu-ally migrate into yours—the *future beside*. Unfortunately, these sandboxes are probably not on your current radar screen, and if you haven't spotted them, they will catch you by surprise when they arrive. Exploring adjacent sandboxes for events that are happening there will enable you to quickly assess the ability of these events to migrate into yours and, more importantly, enable you to take actions to manage and/or control these events to your advantage.

An example is what recently happened to McDonald's. A man in Vermont who has developed cancer claims that his disease was caused by his daily intake of the fat in that chain's hamburgers. Maybe that's why they have announced lower-fat french fries. If we were with Kentucky Fried Chicken (KFC), which is in an adjacent fast-food sandbox, we would start tracking the event at McDonald's because it will eventually migrate its way into our sandbox.

PepsiCo's CEO, Steve Reinemund, announced a goal of making at least 50 percent of the company's products "nutritious." Do you think PepsiCo may have glanced into the McDonald's sandbox?

Exploring adjacent sandboxes for events that are happening there will enable you to quickly assess the ability of these events to migrate into yours and, more importantly, enable you to take actions to manage and/or control these events to your advantage.

Five Places to Look for the Future

It is in these five places—the *futures ahead, beyond, behind, around,* and *beside*—that the future stalks and may spring into your sandbox and catch you unprepared. Or, if you look, you may discover opportunities that others have not yet recognized. And that brings us to a wise quote from one of our clients: "You cannot predict the future, but you can prepare for and control the future."

OBSTACLE 4. STRATEGIZING FOR ADEQUACY, NOT SUPREMACY

What is your strategy engineered to achieve? Just "getting by" or establishing your organization at the pinnacle of a new sandbox you create for yourself?

The fourth obstacle to developing game changing strategies arises when leaders develop strategies for adequacy, not supremacy. Organizations that reluctantly stumble through the annual planning cycle will end up with a strategy that is OK at best. Going through the motions will deliver adequacy, not supremacy.

A Successful Strategy Doesn't Change

If you feel a need to constantly change your business strategy, in our opinion that's a clear signal that "you ain't got one." A successful strategy doesn't change with every gust of competitive or environmental wind that brushes across your sandbox. A successful strategy works to the benefit of a company over a long period of time. In fact, the litmus test of a successful strategy is its longevity.

One would think from reading the business publications that companies come and go according to some preordained law of commerce that dictates that companies rise and fall according to certain events, cycles, or trends. It is easy to understand why one could come to that conclusion. These publications overflow with stories of failed companies. In the last couple of decades, these have included Polaroid, DEC, Enron, Lucent, MCI (formerly WorldCom), and more recently Kodak.

With over 35 years of work in the area of business strategy with the CEOs and executive teams of over 1,000 companies in 30 countries, we have come to a different conclusion. In our view, the difference between companies that succeed over the long term and those that fail and disappear is that successful leadership engages in a process we call *Strategic Thinking*. In other words, long-term successful companies have CEOs and senior executives who are better strategic thinkers than companies that fail. Failure, in our humble opinion, is a self-inflicted wound.

The single most important element common to companies that attain long-term success as opposed to those that fail is this: they have a clear, coherent strategy that they pursue with singularity of purpose that is infused throughout the organization. They have total dedication to it and no deviation from it. Simply put, they have a better strategy that strives for supremacy in their sandbox. However, in our view, one must have supremacy of thinking before one can achieve supremacy of strategy. This is how leaders out-think, not out-muscle, their competitors. As Dwight Eisenhower said, "Wars are won in the planning room, not on the battlefield."

Supremacy, Not Adequacy, Is the Sole Objective of a Long-Term Strategy

What do 3M, Intel, Walmart, Home Depot, Microsoft, Dell, Apple, Oracle, Schwab, E*TRADE, Amazon.com, FedEx, Caterpillar, IBM, General Electric, Nokia, Progressive Insurance, Canon, Sony, Disney, and Southwest Airlines have in common? These different companies have, or had at one point, CEOs who had one trait in common: a grasp of the concepts of strategy, strategic thinking, and competitive supremacy.

In other words, their goal was not to have a strategy that allowed their companies to compete adequately but rather a strategy that aimed at supremacy over their competitors. Supremacy, not adequacy, is the ultimate goal of strategy.

These companies were all influenced at some point in time— usually during their infancy—by a CEO who conceived a clear strategy, with its intent being long-term supremacy in its chosen sandbox. The following are some examples:

- Chubb's intent to dominate the "insurance needs of the well-to-do"
- Boeing's intent to "be the world's preeminent aerospace company"
- Coca-Cola's intent to be the "foremost global beverage company"
- Diebold's intent to dominate the "financial transaction device" market
- Schwab's intent to be the "sole financial advisor to the independent investor"

- Microsoft's intent to be the "primary provider of software in the world"
- Southwest Airlines' intent to be the world's best airline, with its strategy of "One mission: Low fares"

On the other hand, several companies that ran into serious trouble and disappeared or are today in poor health have failed due to poor strategic decisions made by a previous CEO many years ago. The following are some examples, among many:

- Polaroid refused to accept the fact that Sony's introduction of the Mavica digital camera in 1984 was a death threat to Edwin Land's strategy of "instant photography."
- Exxon's foray in the 1980s into the foreign world of office equipment almost led to its downfall. Fortunately, Exxon was smart enough to recognize its mistake and made the right decision to exit that business a few years later.
- Daimler-Benz attempted to become the "world's best managed company" by acquiring a host of "basket-case" companies, none of which were related to cars. This strategy almost put that company out of business.

Another threat to long-term supremacy comes from a totally different source, from left field. This is the advent of a competitor that isn't even on your radar screen.

OBSTACLE 5. FAILING TO LOOK FOR DISRUPTIVE STEALTH COMPETITORS

The fifth obstacle to developing a game changing strategy is thinking about conventional competition only and not considering possible disrupters in the industry. For 25 years, we at DPI have been preaching the need to *change the rules* if a company aspires to establish supremacy over its competitors. However, in the last decade, we have come to the conclusion that changing the rules is not enough. In this competitive era, one must now *change the game itself.* Looking at traditional competitors is not enough. You need to look at potential disrupters in your business arena.

We have discovered four, so far, different forms of tactics that can be used to *change the game:*

Tactics That Change the Game

- Changing enough rules to make a response by competitors impossible
- Turning a competitor's unique strength into a unique weakness
- Making the competitor's strategy redundant
- Changing how customers buy and companies compete

In his recent article "Disrupt or be Disrupted" in the South African newspaper the *Times,* Toby Shapshak observed that industries are being disrupted in response to the news that Kodak, which sold the first Kodak camera in 1888, had filed for Chapter 11. Shapshak's point was that Kodak could have avoided its demise if it had been the disrupter, not the disrupted. He wrote, "Kodak was the first company to make a digital camera, in 1975. It was killed by its own invention, which it spectacularly failed to capitalize on."

Sony capitalized on that invention, and when Sony introduced the world's first Mavica digital camera in May 1984, Polaroid's and Kodak's days were numbered. On that day, Polaroid's concept of instant photography was made redundant. It took Polaroid a couple of years to accept this reality and file for Chapter 11. Kodak's decision to pursue a dual approach to analog and digital strategy was made redundant. It took Kodak 27 years to realize its model could not compete, and it filed for Chapter 11 in January 2012. Kodak has now decided to base its future strategy on printer devices. Will this work? Who are they up against? HP and Canon who have dominated this sandbox for decades. The next couple of years will reveal if Kodak has made the right choice.

In his article, Shapshak wrote:

> Of all the so-called digital disruptions, this has been arguably the most painful. . . . [I]n the last week there were other, much more hyped announcements that imperiled other age-old businesses ripe for similar disruptions.
>
> Apple announced its much-hyped assault on school textbooks—a multi-billion-dollar industry—with a combination of an iPad (obviously, as Apple always drives sales of its hardware, like it did with its iPods and music) and the software to create visually stunning, interactive, video-rich textbooks. . . . These are the study guides for the twenty-first century, where this generation of digital natives are more likely to use tablets than personal computers or any of the other outdated twentieth-century technology we're all still so nostalgic about. That includes good old paper books. Until the Kindle and other e-readers arrived, they were the best delivery mechanism available for dispensing literature or history textbooks. . . .
>
> The publishing industry is ripe for disruption—and the book publishers especially are on notice, having seen what the self-publishing might of Amazon's Kindle store offers. As the famous maxim goes, "You have to cannibalize your own business before someone else does."

We cannot agree with this maxim more. You have to look beyond the conventional competitive environment and look at what may disrupt your business arena. This competitive force we have named the *Stealth Competitor*. This competitor or disrupter has the ability to enter an industry and dramatically change the way the game gets played in an industry.

There are many other examples in industries where the Stealth Competitor has wreaked havoc. Canon did it to Xerox, Walmart did it to the retail industry in the United States and now in other geographic markets like South Africa, and Amazon .com did it too, to Barnes & Noble and Borders, by changing the way consumers access goods and services.

The assumption that your industry cannot be "disrupted" could prove fatal. Numerous existing technologies could spawn new stealth entrants in currently unforeseen ways. Kevin Surace of Serious Energy (formerly Serious Materials), for example, has created a stealth entrant into the venerable world of building materials with a disruptive product, the iWindow. Many new commercialization opportunities await the remarkable new nanomaterial called *graphene*. Another excellent example is 3D printing and the inevitable consequences it will bring to many in manufacturing and even medical industries. A woman just received a new jawbone made through 3D printing technology. 3D what? Could this be a disrupter or create the next Stealth Competitors in your industry?

According to an entry on Wikipedia:

> *3D printing* is a term used to describe the process of creating three-dimensional objects from digital files using a materials printer. The process is similar to printing images on paper. 3D printing is closely associated with additive manufacturing technology, where an object is created by laying down successive layers of material. The term is increasingly being used to describe all types of additive manufacturing processes, or even other types of rapid prototyping technology.
>
> Since 2003 there has been large growth in the sale of 3D printers, which has also driven the cost of 3D printers down. 3D printing technology also finds use in the fields of jewelry, footwear, industrial design, architecture, engineering and construction (AEC), automotive, aerospace, dental and medical industries, education, geographic information systems, civil engineering, and many others.

To our way of thinking, any robust strategy process must consider and paint a picture of potential Stealth Competitors. DPI's Stealth Competitor Process enables leaders to flush out these hidden threats. Peter Doyle, who was the group CEO of Metropolitan Holding in South Africa for 29 years, commented:

> One of the parts of the DPI strategy process is a module called *Stealth Competitors.* By envisioning the characteristics of the business arena of the future, one of Metropolitan's teams was able to envision what new Stealth Competitors might look like. In creating these models, the team discovered some aspects that led to new ventures within Metropolitan. I think it's a very good concept. It frees you up to think completely alternative thoughts.

But no matter how well you have defined the Future Business Arena or thought through and developed a supremacy strategy, implementation of the decisions taken will not materialize unless a very important step is taken.

OBSTACLE 6. FAILING TO GAIN STRATEGIC BUY-IN, WHICH SOMETIMES LEADS TO STRATEGIC TERRORISM

The sixth obstacle to framing a game changing strategy is that leaders cannot get the team on board. Strategic management is a dynamic process that encompasses all facets of business. Effective decision making and strategic thinking are required to determine which steps need to be taken to gain a competitive advantage in the marketplace, and they must be flexible enough to meet the demands of a continually changing environment.

It is the function of all levels of management to be involved in strategic matters, including environmental scanning and analysis, trend forecasts, and competitor analysis so as to make better decisions, especially in times of instability. Too often business strategies are monopolized by the CEO.

As management attempts to implement the business strategy, the organization's operations begin to lack clear direction as they find themselves alienated from the chief executive officer's strategic vision, if they even know what it is. The by-product of the autocratic decision making is that employees fail to gain ownership of the business strategy, leading to underperformance, a lack of motivation, and even resentment toward the company.

As a result of the failure to involve staff in the strategic decision-making process, employees begin to develop an us-versus-them mentality, thereby eroding any positive relationship between the various levels. Without these relationships, morale begins to fade and productivity decreases. Since the employees have been isolated from the decision-making process, their inadequate understanding of the business strategy becomes evident as the implementation is rolled out. Often the only tool available to attempt to align their understanding is the traditional approach involving complex reports that are often poorly understood and difficult to implement. As a result, momentum is lost and resources are wasted. We therefore end up with *strategic terrorism*. This is a term we use to describe the behavior of managers when they don't believe in something; they will find all the reasons or excuses not to support it. Implementation then never happens.

OBSTACLE 7. CONFUSING STRATEGY FORMULATION AND EXECUTION

The seventh obstacle arises when leaders perceive the lack of execution as an execution rather than a formulation issue. Execution is never a trivial endeavor. Turning an agreed-upon strategy into tangible market, product, and customer positions is hard work. However, we have come to the conclusion that when facing difficulties, many leaders are quick to jump to the conclusion that "execution is the problem" rather than looking closer to home in terms of the strategy that has been set and the process that was used to develop it. The process used is a critical determinant in getting acceptance of the agreed-upon strategy. It is the most important aspect, followed by the ability to make the required resources available to enable execution. To put it another way, a poor strategy, or one that nobody understands or agrees with, will struggle to deliver results however good the "execution system."

What is needed then is a critical thinking process that allows the management team to jointly devise a strategy, debate key issues, and evaluate the internal and external environments the organization may face. It is essential to success that there be a systematic, proven process to organize the thinking of this new team and drive their rationale through to meaningful conclusions.

Our extensive experience shows that the facilitator of the process must be a highly experienced, objective outsider. This enables the participants to work on a level playing field, and it ensures that the CEO's thinking does not dominate the debate. Team decision making allows employees to feel they are part of the strategy and part of the organization, and the team will therefore develop interest in the strategy's success. The responsibility of the business strategy shifts from resting with an individual to resting with the team. With this group-oriented approach, each member of this carefully selected team is actively involved in detailing and developing the company's business concept, thus leading to a far greater command of the strategies involved. Improved insight into the strategy allows for the boundaries to be set and maintained, the deliverables to be met, and the business plan to be successfully completed.

Together a team is able to develop a meaningful strategic profile for the future of the company that every member can agree upon, as well as an action plan to ensure effective implementation of the strategy. But how do we draw the line between thinking and planning?

OBSTACLE 8. FAILING TO RESOURCE THE IMPLEMENTATION OF THE STRATEGY

The final obstacle arises when leaders fail to resource the strategy deployment appropriately and effectively.

Developing and implementing a wonderful strategy that will clearly change the game in a new sandbox you create for yourself, and to which the entire organization is fully committed, will not, in themselves, ensure the strategy's succeess. For it to succeed, the implementation of the strategy must be properly resourced.

Financial resources are certainly an element of this, but cash is not the only prerequisite for smooth implementation. Transformative leaders will avoid the following pitfalls:

- *Failure to drive implementation passionately.* In our experience real leaders who are genuinely convinced and passionate about the strategy will drive it relentlessly and talk about it in tangible and relevant terms, and its implications, at every opportunity, to anyone and everyone, regardless of his or her level or position. It is a living, breathing strategy; it is not a thick file gathering dust while sitting on the shelf.
- *Failure to adequately resource strategic implementation projects.* Budgets for strategy implementation need to be calculated and funded.
- *Failure to resource management time.* Do not assume that fully stretched execs, working 10 to 12 hours a day, can manage the implementation of the strategy between three and five o'clock in the morning!
- *Failure to equip the rank and file.* As discussed in Chapter 9, strategy implementation will require superior decision-making skills throughout the entire organization.

WHAT IS STRATEGIC THINKING? A DEEPER LOOK

Strategic thinking, to us, is the type of thinking that goes on in the heads of the CEO and the management team, that attempts to transform the conceptual and abstract vision into a working and dynamic tool that we call a *strategic profile*. In fact, strategic thinking is akin to picture painting, whereby the executives of an organization literally "draw" a picture or profile of what they want the business to look like at some point in the future.

Why should the management team take time to do this? How will this effort help the organization?

The answer is simple. Such a profile will give the organization's employees a target to help them make consistent and logical decisions over time. People can then pursue decisions and plans that fall within the "frame" of the picture and avoid pursuing those that fall outside that frame. (See Figure 3.8.)

FIGURE 3.8 **STRATEGIC PROFILE AS A TARGET**

Strategic
Profile

Strategic
Plan

Why?

Operational
Plan

DETERMINING THE FUTURE STRATEGIC PROFILE OF THE BUSINESS

How do we go about describing the *future strategic profile* for an organization? An organization's profile is found in four basic traits. Just as a person's profile is made up of eyes, ears, nose, and mouth, an organization's profile is found in four areas—(1) products and services, (2) customers and users, (3) industry and market segments, and (4) geographic markets. (See Figure 3.9.)

Everything else that goes on in an organization is either an input to this profile (such as capital, manufacturing processes, and distribution systems) or an output from this profile (such as margins, profits, and dividends).

However, strategic thinking goes one step further: identifying the products and services, customers and users, industry and market segments, and geographic markets upon which the company should place more emphasis, as well as those upon which it should place less emphasis. (See Figure 3.10.)

FIGURE 3.9 **STRATEGIC PROFILE COMPONENTS**

Products and Services

Customers and Users

Industry and Market Segments

Geographic Markets

FIGURE 3.10 | FUTURE STRATEGIC PROFILE FOCUS

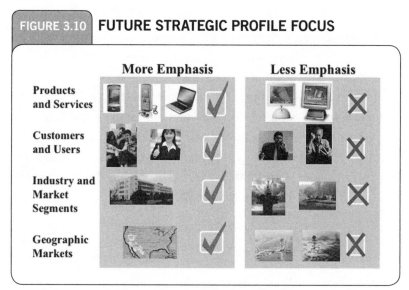

Strategically, it is often more important to know what the strategy or vision *does not* lend itself to than it is to know to what it *does*. The reason for this is that management personnel perform two critical tasks that set the direction of the organization and influence its eventual look.

First, executives allocate resources. Allocating resources strategically means giving more resources to the areas of the future strategic profile that the company wants to emphasize. In other words, activities that will bring in products and services, customers and users, industry and market segments, and geographic markets that resemble items on the left side of our profile will get preferential treatment. Activities on the right side of the profile will get fewer resources.

Second, and more importantly, executives identify which opportunities the organization *should* be pursuing. The future strategic profile is again the final filter for these choices.

Opportunities that will bring the firm items that resemble the ones on the left side will receive preferential treatment over those that do not. With a profile or vision articulated in this manner and embedded in the heads of all the key people in the organization, we can now start to manage strategically. This vision or strategic profile becomes the ultimate test bed for all decisions made in the organization.

The next question that comes to mind is, "How do we determine the line of demarcation between the items that will receive more emphasis and those that will receive less emphasis in the future?" The answer to this question gives rise to the most important concept of strategic thinking: What determines the strategic heartbeat of the business?

CHAPTER 4

Determining the Strategic Heartbeat of the Business

To achieve a dominant position in its selected sandbox in its industry, a company needs to have a strategy that establishes a significant and sustainable point of differentiation—one that enables it to add unique value that competitors will have difficulty duplicating. Of course, most companies have a strategy of some sort. Yet few are able to create a clear definition of that single differentiating factor—if there is one—that has enabled the company to be successful in the past. Still fewer have looked down the road to create a scenario, or strategy, that will enable them to be successful in the environment they will face in the future.

We call that defining factor the *Driving Force*. It is the component of the business that is unique to that company, and it is the key determinant of the choices management makes with regard to future products, future customers, and future markets. Without an understanding of, and agreement upon, that Driving

Force, management will have a difficult time creating a strategy for the future that will breed supremacy over the company's competitors.

WHAT MAKES YOUR STRATEGY TICK?

The best way to determine whether a CEO and the management team have a strategy is to observe them in meetings as they try to decide whether or not to pursue an opportunity. When we sat in on such meetings, we noticed that management put each opportunity through a hierarchy of different filters. The ultimate filter, however, was always whether there was a fit between the products, customers, and markets that the opportunity brought and one key component of the organization. If they found a fit there, they felt comfortable with that opportunity and would proceed with it. If they did not find a fit there, they would pass.

We also found that different companies, however, looked for different kinds of fit. Some companies looked for a fit between similar products. Others were less concerned about the similarity of products than about a fit with the customer base. Still others were not interested in the similarity of products or of the customer base but rather a fit with the technology involved or a fit with their sales and marketing method, or their distribution system. The following paragraph describes some examples.

What fit was Daimler looking for when it bought Chrysler? Obviously, the fit was one between similar products. Johnson & Johnson (J&J), on the other hand, was looking for an entirely different kind of fit when it acquired Neutrogena creams from one company and the clinical diagnostics laboratories of Kodak, each bringing dramatically different products. J&J was looking for a fit between the class of customers served—doctors, nurses, patients, and mothers—the heartbeat of J&J's strategy. 3M looked for still another fit when choosing opportunities. 3M did not care what the products were or who the customers were.

What 3M did care about was whether there was a fit between the technology that the opportunity required and the technology—polymer chemistry—that lay at the root of 3M's strategy. If the technology fit, then 3M management felt comfortable in pursuing that opportunity.

TEN STRATEGIC AREAS

The next question that came to our minds was this: What are the areas of an organization that cause management to decide how to allocate resources or choose opportunities? We discovered that each of the 1,000-plus companies we had worked with globally consisted of 10 basic components:

1. Every company offered *products or services* for sale.
2. Every company sold its products or services to a certain *class of customer or end user.*
3. These customers or end users always resided in certain *categories of markets.*
4. Every company employed *technology* in its products or services.
5. Every company had a *production* facility located somewhere that had a certain amount of *capacity* or certain in-built *capabilities* in the making of products or services.
6. Every company used certain *sales or marketing methods* to acquire customers for its products or services.
7. Every company employed certain *distribution methods* to get products from its location to its customers' location.
8. Every company made use of *natural resources* to one degree or another.
9. Every company monitored its *size and growth* performance.
10. Every company monitored its *return or profit* performance.

As a result of these observations, two key messages emerged. First, all of those areas exist in every company. Second, and more importantly, one of the areas tends to dominate the strategy of a company consistently over time. It is to favor or leverage this one area of the business time and again that determines how management allocates resources or chooses opportunities. In other words, one component of the business is the engine of the strategy—that company's so-called DNA, or Driving Force. This Driving Force determines the array of products, customers, industries, and geographic markets that management chooses to emphasize more and emphasize less. (See Figures 4.1 and 4.2.)

Hennie Du Plessis, the former CEO of Bytes Healthcare Solutions (BHS) in South Africa, on the subject of Driving Force, said: "When we talked about DPI's concept of the Driving Force, we identified with it intellectually. We thought it was a very interesting way of understanding what our combined businesses were all about, because we had not had that conversation at that point."

FIGURE 4.1 EVERY BUSINESS HAS 10 COMPONENTS . . .

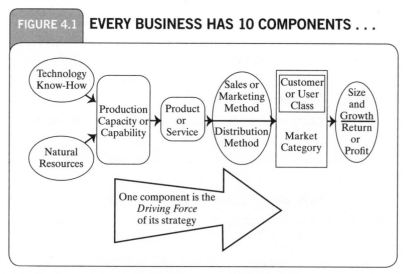

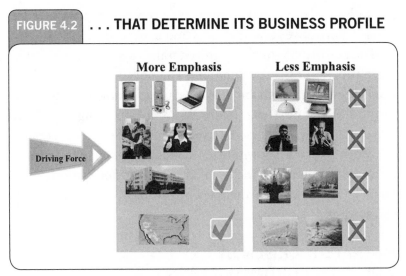

FIGURE 4.2 . . . THAT DETERMINE ITS BUSINESS PROFILE

DEFINITIONS OF DRIVING FORCE

In order to explain this concept more clearly, one needs to look at an organization as a body in motion. Every organization, on any one day, is an organism that has movement and momentum, and it is going forward in some direction. Our thesis is that 1 of the 10 components of a company's operation is the strategic engine behind the decisions that management makes. Some typical examples follow.

A STRATEGY DRIVEN BY A SINGLE PRODUCT OR SERVICE

A *product-driven company* is one that is "locked" into a product concept of some kind whose function and look do not change much over time. Future products are adaptations, modifications, or extensions of the current product. In other words, future product offerings emanating from such a company are derivatives of the existing product, and the existing product is a "genetic" derivative of the original product. Such companies grow by offering new derivatives that fragment and expand the market.

The automobile industry, in general, is a good example. The basic function of the automobile has not changed for a hundred years, and it probably will not change for the next hundred. Toyota, Mercedes-Benz, and VW are all pursuing a product-driven strategy. Other companies following such a concept are Boeing or Airbus with their concept of "flying machines," insurance companies with "insurance" as their product, and Harley-Davidson with its concept of "fulfilling dreams with extraordinary motorcycles."

A STRATEGY DRIVEN BY A USER OR CUSTOMER CLASS

A *user- or customer-class-driven company* is one that has anchored its business around a specific describable class of users or customers (people). The company then identifies a common need of the user or customer class and responds by offering a wide array of genetically unrelated products or services that satisfy this need. To grow, the company continually researches the needs of this user or customer class in order to identify new opportunities. As a result, the scope of the company's products is usually very wide, and the products have little resemblance to each other. However, the user or customer that buys and/or uses these products is constant.

Packaged goods companies and publishers of special-interest magazines are examples of such organizations. Johnson & Johnson's strategy of serving "doctors, nurses, patients, and mothers" with a wide variety of health- and wellness-related products is another example.

A STRATEGY DRIVEN BY MARKET TYPE OR CATEGORY

A *market category–driven company* is very similar to a user- or customer-driven company, except that this company has deliberately anchored its business to a describable category of market and not to the customer or end user. That market, then, is the only one it serves. The firm's strategy is to continuously scrutinize that market in an attempt to identify related needs. Once these needs are found, then appropriate products, which may otherwise be unrelated to each other, are made.

One example is American Hospital Supply (now Allegiance). In its very name, this company has identified the market to which its business is anchored: the hospital. The strategy of the company is to respond to a variety of needs coming from that market. As a result, the product scope of the firm ranges from bedpans to sutures and from gauze pads to electronic imaging systems. These products are unrelated to each other; they are not genetic derivatives. The only common thread is that they are all used in a hospital. Another is Disney's concept of "wholesome entertainment for the family."

A STRATEGY DRIVEN BY TECHNOLOGY OR KNOW-HOW

A *technology-driven company* is a company that has anchored its strategy in the ability to invent or acquire the hard or soft technology or know-how that is at the root of its business. The company has the ability to enhance or acquire new complementary technologies or know-how for which there is no immediate product available. Companies with this drive will then seek out applications in the marketplace for the use of this technology and then transform it into products. Over time such companies get involved in a broad array of products, all of which stem from the particular technology and serve a broad array of customers and market segments.

DuPont, in the synthetic fiber industry with its inventions of nylon and rayon, is a good example. The microprocessor industry, 3M, and South African Synthetic Oils (the Sasol Group) with its oil from coal and natural gases are other good examples of such companies.

A STRATEGY DRIVEN BY PRODUCTION CAPACITY OR CAPABILITY

A *production capacity–driven company* is usually a company that has a substantial investment in its production facility, and the thrust is to keep that facility operating at maximum capacity. The capacity is usually perishable in nature, and thus the organization is driven to offer products that utilize that capacity to its fullest. As a result, its range of products is very wide with the only common thread being the need to keep the production facility full. Historically, pulp and paper companies, steel mills, and oil refineries have fallen into this classification. Service-related companies, such as airlines and hotels, are also often "production capacity" driven.

A *production capability–driven company* is one that has built some unique capabilities into its production process, and it pursues only opportunities that can utilize these unique capabilities that are difficult for its competitors to duplicate. It then looks for opportunities where these capabilities can be exploited. Job shops and specialty printers are examples.

A STRATEGY DRIVEN BY SALES OR MARKETING METHOD

A *company driven by its method of sales or marketing* will have products, customers, and markets that are determined by the uniqueness of its selling approach. Examples of this Driving Force can be found in companies that usually sell "door-to-door," such as some cosmetic companies like Avon, or through house parties like Tupperware, or companies that leverage television time to sell products they can demonstrate, or Amazon.com, whose strategy is to use the Internet to sell a wide array of consumer products.

To illustrate the constraints that the Driving Force places on the nature of the company's products, sales- or marketing method–driven companies would never offer products that cannot be sold and delivered by its selling method due to the size, weight, bulk, or other characteristics of the products.

A STRATEGY DRIVEN BY DISTRIBUTION METHOD

A company whose products, customers, and markets are determined by its method of distribution would be a *distribution method–driven company*. It needs to have ownership of or full control of the specific distribution method. Telephone companies with their vast networks of wires and distribution towers dictate the nature of the products or services they offer their clients. FedEx with its concept of "moving anything, for anyone, anywhere in the world, within 24 hours" is another good example.

A STRATEGY DRIVEN BY NATURAL RESOURCES

When access to, or pursuit of, natural resources becomes the main determining factor for a company's products and markets, then that company is *natural resources driven*. Examples of natural resources–driven companies are the fishing companies, mining companies, timber companies, and water utilities.

A STRATEGY DRIVEN BY SIZE OR GROWTH

Companies that seek size for the sake of size alone are *size or growth driven*. The need to pursue growth in order to have economies of scale dictates the markets they seek and the products they offer. Such companies pursue growth for the sake of growth exclusively. It is the only criterion used to judge any opportunity.

A STRATEGY DRIVEN BY RETURN OR PROFIT

Organizations whose only determinant for entry into a product or market area is *return or profit* fall into this category. Conglomerates are often good examples. They are usually organized along the lines of a corporate control body with fully autonomous subsidiaries with usually few or no links between them except a certain level of profit. Subsidiaries are bought or sold on this criterion alone. Western examples such as Tyco, AlliedSignal, and General Electric are decreasing, but due to different market and political structures, return/profit firms remain prevalent in Asia. Among these are Jardine Matheson (Hong Kong), Keppel Group (Singapore), Fuson International (China), CP Group (Thailand), and Chaebol (Korea).

KEY STRATEGIC QUESTIONS

When we take a client through our Strategic Thinking Process, we have the CEO and the management team debate three key questions to enable them to identify the company's current and future Driving Force:

> Question 1. Which component of your business is currently driving your strategy and has made you look as you look today in terms of current products, customers, and markets?

If there are 10 people in the room, how many answers do you think we get? We get 10 and sometimes more. The reason is simple. Each person has a different perception as to which component of the business is the Driving Force behind the company's strategy. These different interpretations lead to different visions of where the organization is headed. The difficulty, while this is going on, is that each member of the team makes decisions that pull the company left and right, so the company zigzags its way forward without establishing supremacy in any one sandbox. The inevitable result is that resources are wrongly employed.

The methodology we bring to bear at DPI encourages executives to look back at the history of decisions they have made and, by doing so, recognize a pattern. Typically, most of their decisions were made to favor one component of the business. Thus, the executives recognize the current Driving Force behind their current strategy.

Question 2. Which component of the company should be the
Driving Force behind the company's strategy in the future?

This question is more important because it indicates that the
company's future strategy should not simply be an extrapolation
of the current strategy. Any strategy needs to accommodate the
environment the company will encounter in the future, and that
environment could be very different from the one encountered
in the past. This question is the basis for envisioning *breakaway
strategies* that obliterate the assumptions of the current sandbox
to envision a new one that offers significantly greater opportunities to establish supremacy over competitors. Such a strategy
enables the company to create, or reposition itself in, a future
sandbox in a way that offers it more growth and profitability
than competitors and offers it control of that sandbox.

Question 3. What impact will this Driving Force have on the
choices the company must make regarding future products,
future customers, and future markets?

The Driving Force the company chooses as the engine of
its strategy will determine the choices its executives make as to
the products, customers, and markets that they will and will not
emphasize in the future. These choices will shape the profile
of the company, and maybe even the industry, over time. Each
Driving Force will cause management to make very different
choices that will make the company look very different from the
way it looks today. In other words, just as your personal DNA
determines what you look like and why you look different from
other people, the same is true for your corporate DNA. The
component of the company you select as the DNA of its strategy
will determine what that company will eventually look like and
why it will look different from its competitors.

Bernard Sorel, former managing director of BN/Bombardier
Eurorail, said:

The concepts of the Driving Force and Controlling the Sandbox have become part of our modus operandi. Three times (twice at Caterpillar and once at BN), I have noted that the concept of the Driving Force in the DPI process enabled the management team to articulate a clear statement of strategy, clear strategic objectives, and a short list of Critical Issues that allowed the company to manage its resources more effectively. The process helps management aim its resources at strategic targets, avoiding dispersion and waste of energy.

ARTICULATING THE BUSINESS CONCEPT

The Driving Force concept is a tool to allow executives to identify which area of the business is at the root of their company's products, customers, and markets and is strategically more important to that company than any other area.

However, it is also a tool to allow executives to articulate their concept of doing business in that mode. Every business is founded on a concept of some kind. We now need to formulate a one-paragraph statement that explains how this component is the heartbeat of the business and how it will propel or drive the organization and dictate its behavior in the choice of future products, markets, and customers. This statement will be the conceptual underpinning of the business.

Alfred P. Sloan, who was the CEO of General Motors in the first half of this century, put it this way in his book *My Years with General Motors*:

Every enterprise needs a concept of its industry. There is a logical way of doing business in accordance with the facts and circumstances of an industry, if you can figure it out. If there are different concepts among the enterprises involved, these concepts are likely to express competitive forces in their most vigorous and most decisive forms.

As Sloan described, in crafting this statement it is imperative to avoid ending up with a meaningless mission. *Meaningless mission statements* are so general that they possess the seemingly unfathomable ability to get everyone to agree to something that nobody understands.

Here is one example: "We are a successful, growing company dedicated to achieving superior results by ensuring that our actions are aligned with shareholder expectations. Our primary mission is to create value for our shareholders."

And another beauty: "Our mission is to provide products and services of superior competitive quality and value, to achieve strong growth in sales and income, to realize consistently higher returns on equity and cash required to fuel our growth, and to have people who contribute superior performance at all levels."

Those statements are as meaningless as they are useless when used as filters to make decisions. They fall apart because they allow everything through. Nothing is eliminated.

"Increasing shareholder value . . ." by doing what? By making what products? By selling to which customers? By concentrating on which market segments? By pursuing which geographic markets?

Without answers to those questions, how can someone be expected to allocate resources properly and choose the appropriate opportunities to pursue? No wonder so many of the Fortune 500 companies have lost large chunks of their markets and have had to engage in massive downsizing programs.

Our view on the subject of strategy statements is simple:

- A good business or strategic concept should not be longer than a paragraph or two. There is no need to have pages and pages describing what the business is about. However, every word, modifier, or qualifier must be carefully thought through because each moves the line of demarcation between the products, customers, and markets that will receive more emphasis and those that will receive less.

- It is our opinion that the ability of people to execute a CEO's strategy is inversely proportional to the length of the statement.

Therefore, the statement must be precise and concise. The Driving Force concept explained above is a tool that allows management to identify which area of the business is at the root of the company's products, customers, and markets and is strategically more important to that company than any other area. However, it is also a tool that allows management to articulate their concept of doing business in that mode.

Depending on which Driving Force is chosen, the organization's business concept or strategy will be dramatically different. Even when different companies have the same Driving Force, they may still have business concepts different enough from each other to be going in different directions. Some good examples are found in the automobile industry: Volvo, BMW, Mercedes, and Volkswagen can all be said to be product driven: they produce only automobiles. However, each of these companies has a very different conception of its products:

- Volvo makes "safe and durable cars."
- Mercedes makes the "best engineered cars."
- BMW makes "sheer driving pleasure cars."
- Volkswagen makes the "people's cars."

As a result, each of these companies goes down a slightly different road and seldom competes with the others even though they all make a similar product—a car.

EXAMPLES OF STRATEGIC BUSINESS CONCEPTS

The following are examples of business concepts that we have helped our client organizations to construct. For reasons of confidentiality, the names of the companies involved have been omitted.

Example 1

Our strategy is to market, manufacture, and distribute saw blade products, made from strip metal stock, that provide exceptional value.

We will concentrate on high-performance, material separation applications where we can leverage our integrated manufacturing capabilities to develop customized, innovative, consumable products with demonstrable advantages that bring premium prices.

We will seek out customer segments and geographic markets where the combination of superior distribution and technical support services will give us an additional competitive advantage.

Example 2

Our strategy is to provide reinsurance products to assist organizations in managing life, health, and annuity risks.

We will differentiate ourselves by leveraging our mortality and morbidity risk management expertise.

We will concentrate on market segments where we can establish and maintain a leadership position.

We will concentrate in growth-oriented, "free" geographic areas with reliable databases and predictable risk patterns where we can achieve critical mass and a balanced portfolio.

Example 3

We proactively seek out the building, repair, and remodeling needs of professional tradespeople in the commercial and residential construction industry.

We respond with cost-effective, differentiated staple products that enhance the performance or ease the installation of key building materials and are category leaders.

We concentrate in geographic markets with a significant and/or growing construction industry and an adequate distribution infrastructure to reach a critical mass of end users.

Our intent is to be the recognized leader in the products we offer.

Example 4

Our strategy is to fulfill the complete spectrum of healthcare needs of cancer patients and their families.

We respond with treatment options that truly make a difference, delivered by the ablest professionals in a seamless and sensitive manner that empowers patients to make coherent decisions.

We will concentrate on geographic markets in which we can develop competitive advantage with all constituencies involved in the continuum of cancer care.

Our intent is to be the recognized leader in providing positive, measurable outcomes.

KEEPING THE STRATEGY STRONG AND HEALTHY

As we observed companies over the years, we noted that there were some that could perpetuate their strategy successfully over long periods of time. In the same industries, others had great difficulty doing that, and their performance level over time resembled that of a yo-yo. What, we asked, was the difference?

Over time, the strategy of an organization can, like a person, get stronger and healthier or weaker and sicker. What determines, in our opinion, which way it will go is what we call the *Areas of Excellence* that a company deliberately cultivates over time to keep the strategy strong and healthy and to give it an edge in the marketplace. An *Area of Excellence*, another key concept of strategic thinking, is a describable skill or capability that a company has cultivated to a level of proficiency greater than anything else it does and, particularly, better than anyone else does. It is a strategic capability in two or three key areas that keeps the strategy alive and working.

DETERMINING THE STRATEGIC CAPABILITIES THAT AMPLIFY COMPETITIVE ADVANTAGE

The concept of identifying the Areas of Excellence that the company needs to cultivate to make its strategy succeed is critical because they vary greatly from one Driving Force to another.

A STRATEGY DRIVEN BY PRODUCT OR SERVICE

A product-driven company survives on the quality of its products or services. It has to invest in the research and development of its products and process development in order to produce better products than any other competitor in the market. It then has to support the products it offers to the market with after-sales service. In a product-driven mode, you maintain your competitive advantage by cultivating excellence in *product development* and *service*.

A STRATEGY DRIVEN BY CUSTOMER OR USER CLASS OR A STRATEGY DRIVEN BY MARKET CATEGORY

An organization that is user class or market category driven must also cultivate excellence to optimize its competitive advantage, but in dramatically different areas. A company that has a user-class or market category drive has placed its destiny in the hands of the user class or the market category. Therefore, to survive and prosper, it must know its user class or market category better than any competitor. The company must have timely information in order to quickly detect any changes in habits, demographics, likes, and dislikes. It then has to cultivate the means over time to build customer loyalty to the company's products or brands. In a user-class or market category–driven mode, you amplify your competitive advantage by cultivating excellence in *user or market research* and *loyalty.*

A STRATEGY DRIVEN BY PRODUCTION CAPACITY OR CAPABILITY

A production capacity–driven strategy requires lower production costs because these companies are normally driven by commodity prices in the market such as pulp prices, gold prices, or timber prices. These prices are normally set by the traders on the global commodity markets. The company will be a price taker, and not a price maker, for the raw materials that go into their products. They have to drive efficiencies in their manufacturing plants to drive lower costs of production to improve margins. A second requirement that has a direct effect on the lower costs of production is *substitute marketing.* Capacity-driven companies need to be good at substituting what comes off their machines for other things. Paper companies will look at substituting newspaper with paper plates, toilet paper, paper towels, and so forth.

A production capability–driven company is one that has built special capabilities into its production process that allow it to make products with features that are difficult for its competitors to duplicate. It then looks for opportunities where these capabilities can be exploited. Job shops and specialty printers are examples. As a result, these companies are always looking to add to or enhance these distinctive production capabilities because therein resides their competitive advantage.

In a production capacity– or capability-driven mode, you drive your competitive advantage by cultivating excellence in *manufacturing efficiency* and *substitute marketing.*

A STRATEGY DRIVEN BY TECHNOLOGY OR KNOW-HOW

A company that is technology or know-how driven uses technology or know-how as the edge. Thus, an Area of Excellence required to win under this strategy is research, either basic or applied. By pushing the technology further than any other competitor, new products and new markets will emerge. Technology and know-how companies usually create markets rather than respond to needs, and they usually follow their technology wherever it leads them. The second area that is essential is that of finding applications for the technology and know-how. These companies seem to have a knack for finding a variety of applications for their technology that call for highly differentiated products. In a technology- or know-how-driven mode, you strengthen your competitive advantage by cultivating excellence in *research* and *application marketing.*

A STRATEGY DRIVEN BY SALES OR MARKETING METHOD

The prosperity of a sales- or marketing method–driven company depends on the reach and effectiveness of its selling method. As a result, the first strategic skill it must cultivate is the ongoing recruitment of salespeople. The second strategic skill needed to succeed with this strategy is improving the effectiveness of the selling method. Constant training in product knowledge, product demonstrations, and selling skills is vital. In a sales- or marketing method–driven mode, you increase your competitive advantage by cultivating excellence in *salespeople recruitment* and *selling effectiveness.*

A STRATEGY DRIVEN BY DISTRIBUTION METHOD

To win the war while pursuing a distribution method–driven strategy, you must first of all have the most effective distribution method. As a result, you must offer products and services that use or enhance your distribution system. Second, you must always look for ways to optimize the effectiveness, either in cost or value, of that system. That is your edge. In a distribution method–driven mode, you amplify your competitive advantage by cultivating excellence in *system effectiveness* and *system organization.*

A STRATEGY DRIVEN BY NATURAL RESOURCES

Successful natural resources–driven companies excel at exploring and finding the types of resources their companies rely on. Once access to the resources is secured, you need to convert those resources into end products that the market requires at acceptable margins. In a natural resources–driven mode, you maintain your competitive advantage by cultivating excellence in *exploration* and *converting.*

A STRATEGY DRIVEN BY SIZE OR GROWTH

Achieving critical mass or market share size to drive economies of scale requires the maximization of volumes in the selected market. Opportunities to grow will be sought either through market development or acquisitions to ensure that the company achieves its growth objectives. The second skill required is the ability to manage the assets that the company is required to grow. This will ensure that the business does not lose ground in either the products or markets in which it seeks growth. In a size/growth-driven mode, you strengthen your competitive advantage by cultivating excellence in *volume maximization* and *asset management.*

A STRATEGY DRIVEN BY RETURN OR PROFIT

Companies that choose a return/profit-driven strategy require excellence in financial management. One such area is *portfolio management.* This means proficiency at moving assets around in order to maximize the return and/or profit of the entire organization. A second area of excellence is *information systems.* These companies usually have a corporate "Big Brother" group that constantly monitors the performance of the various divisions. As soon as a problem is detected, an attempt to correct or expunge it is made. In a return/profit-driven mode, you amplify your competitive advantage by cultivating excellence in *portfolio management* and *information systems.*

Why is this concept of an Area of Excellence an integral part of strategic thinking? Each Driving Force brings with it a requirement to excel in a very different set of skills. No company has the resources to develop skills equally in all strategic areas that accompany each Driving Force. Therefore, strategic decision making relies on management's ability to clearly identify those two or three skills that are critical to the success of their strategy, and they give those areas preferential resources. In good times, these areas receive additional resources; in bad times, they are the last areas to cut.

CHAPTER 5

The Strategic Thinking Process: From Strategy Formulation to Deployment

DPI provided outstanding support at a critical point in the evolution of one of our key businesses in China. The discipline and rigor of the DPI process coupled with the valuable business acumen of the DPI China team enabled us to efficiently and effectively develop a new 10-year business strategy. As a result, both the company and the team regained the confidence needed to capture the opportunities present in the highly challenging and competitive China market.

—JOHN LEPORE, CHAIR, GLAXOSMITHKLINE (CHINA) INVESTMENT CO., LTD.

The word *process* is often heard in business circles, so one would think that the meaning of that word is well understood. Our experience at DPI does not show that to be true. In fact, we have noticed that there are several different words used to connote that a process is in place: *system, method, procedure, protocol, formula,* and *practice.* Our intent is not to attempt to define each of these words but to describe our definition of the word *process.* In fact, in order to define the word, one needs to understand the meaning of the word *concept.*

At DPI, we define *concept* as an idea or premise that explains a certain phenomenon or behavior. These would include the following examples:

- Driving Force
- Area of Excellence
- Controlling the Sandbox
- Stealth Competitor

A *process,* on the other hand, is the assemblage of a number of concepts, or steps, into a logical sequence that allows a person to use the process more effectively. In other words, a *process* is a series of *codified concepts.*

However, in any organization, there are two types of processes at work. We call these *hard* and *soft processes.*

Hard processes are easily codified because they can easily be detected and their sequence of steps can be traced and drawn as a flowchart. These would include processes or systems that exist in most organizations, such as the following:

- Capital expenditure requests
- Personnel recruitment procedures
- Customer complaint reports
- Procurement protocols

Soft processes occur in the minds of people and are a reflection of their thinking. These thinking processes are much more difficult to codify because they occur inside a person's mind—not an easy place to probe. However, at DPI, that is our forte. Our Area of Excellence is the ability to codify *critical thinking processes* that improve a company's ability to formulate and deploy a distinctive strategy; create strategic, new-to-the-market products; and manage strategic information more effectively.

These processes have been developed by participating in real work sessions with hundreds of CEOs and their management teams when we discuss such topics as strategy and product development. By listening to their conversations, we have discovered certain "concepts" that seem to be at the root of those discussions. Seeing a concept being employed, usually because the staff members have absorbed it by osmosis, by several companies helps us to discern a certain pattern of thinking, and the concept is validated. We then organize these concepts into a logical sequence, or "process," complete with a series of unique questions, which can then be used consciously by the management of any company, which in turn will enable them to make decisions by design, and not by accident.

Chung Chee Kit, director of IMC Corp., commented on the strength of a process developed in the DPI way: "This process's strength is not in theory (which we have enough of) but in real implementation."

The first and foremost responsibility of any CEO or leader is to formulate a strategy for the organization in order to give its employees a sense of direction and harness their energy toward the goal of supremacy over the company's competitors. The process that assists a CEO in this endeavor is the *Strategic Thinking Process*, which is proprietary to DPI. The following is an overview of how the process proceeds.

PHASE 1. INTRODUCTION AND OVERVIEW

This first phase is a half-day introductory session with two activities. First, we give the participants an overview of the concepts and process so that they are comfortable with these. The second activity is to introduce our *Strategic Input Survey*, in which the participants are asked to respond to a set of questions about various aspects of the company prior to the main three-day session that follows a month later. Their answers become the "raw material" for the next session. These responses are sent to us for editing and collating. Our goal is to encourage thoughtful attention to these key questions and extract meaningful answers as opposed to simply brainstorming answers on the spur of the moment.

PHASE 2. STRATEGIC THINKING SESSION

This is a three-day breakaway session with the senior management team of the organization. The diagram in Figure 5.1 shows the work covered during the main thinking session with a client.

The session starts on the first day with the construction of a "snapshot" of the company in its present form. This consists of identifying the characteristics that are common to all

FIGURE 5.1 STRATEGIC THINKING PROCESS

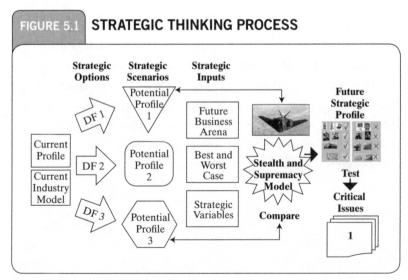

of the company's products, all of the company's customers, all of the company's market segments, and all of the company's geographic markets. By identifying the characteristics that are common across these four elements of a company's profile, we can then uncover the company's current Driving Force (DF), its current business concept, and its current Areas of Excellence. Gaining agreement about the company's current profile is the starting point of strategy formulation.

The next step in this process is to construct the industry model the organization currently finds itself in to determine how the game is being played. This is an important step in order to "change the game," or sandbox, to one's advantage. Therefore, the following questions need to be answered:

- How is the game played today?
- Who are the participants in this sandbox?
- Which entity is in control of the rules in this sandbox?
- Which entity influences the rules in this sandbox?
- Which companies are at the mercy of those mentioned above?
- What can we do to upset their control or influence?

The next step in the process is to conduct a scan of the external environment and determine what the Future Business Arena in which we will find ourselves will look like. Once we are reasonably comfortable with that picture of the future, we can more specifically identify the strategic variables that will play for or against us in that arena. This will help us circumscribe the sandbox over which we want to establish supremacy.

The final step on the first day is to agree on the strategic variables that will play for and against the organization in determining its future response to the changing of the playing field conditions.

On the second day, the first step is to identify which components of our business could be the Driving Force of our future strategy as well as potential *Stealth Competitors*.

Our clients have found the creation of a Stealth Competitor to be both fun and potentially transforming. By knowing how the game is currently being played in a given industry and who is setting the rules, we can ask which Stealth Competitor could step into that sandbox and attempt to establish supremacy for itself and create havoc for us by changing the game. One team is given this assignment, and they develop a specific strategy and business model that such a stealth entrant would deploy against us with the intent of gaining supremacy.

While that is happening, we discuss which Driving Force could be the engine of the organization's future strategy. We have seen that companies can usually identify two or three areas that could be the engine of their future strategy. We then take each of these "possible" Driving Forces and develop *profiles* of what we would emphasize more or emphasize less under each one. The development of these scenarios allows the CEO and the management team to choose the Driving Force that will best deal with all current competitors, as well as any new stealth entrant into our sandbox.

The final day of this work session focuses on bringing to the surface the Critical Issues that the management team will need to address and resolve over time in order to attain, maintain, or enhance supremacy in the chosen sandbox.

IDENTIFICATION OF CRITICAL ISSUES

Critical Issues are the bridge between the current profile and the future strategic profile of an organization that management has deliberately decided to pursue. The direction of the organization has been decided, and managing that direction begins. Managing that direction on an ongoing basis means management of the Critical Issues that stem from four key areas (see Figure 5.2):

- Structure
- Systems and processes

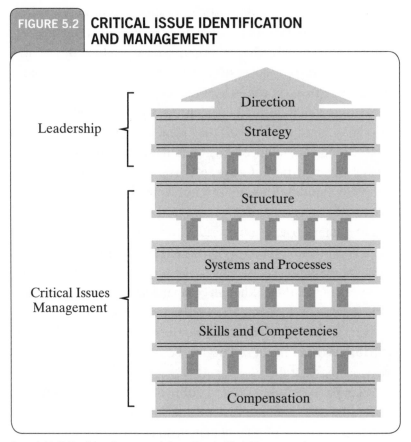

FIGURE 5.2 CRITICAL ISSUE IDENTIFICATION AND MANAGEMENT

Leadership
- Direction
- Strategy

Critical Issues Management
- Structure
- Systems and Processes
- Skills and Competencies
- Compensation

- Skills and competencies
- Compensation

Critical Issues That Relate to Structure

One of our clients recently asked us a very good question: "Since most corporations are organized in a similar manner, does that mean that they have a similar strategy?"

After all, most companies have a marketing function, a sales function, a production function, an engineering function, an accounting function, an IT function, a human resources function, and so on. Most are also organized in a similar manner geographically, with a domestic operational unit and an international unit organized by country, or groups of countries, into regions. They may further be organized by product, by country, which leads to some form of *matrix organization*. Therefore, a similar organization would seem to lead to a similar strategy.

Nothing could be further from the truth! Although organizational structures look as if they stem from the same business model, important nuances exist that make the various functions behave in very different ways. A correlating example is people. Although men often wear suits and women often wear dresses, no two women or two men behave in the same way.

The same is true in business. Although all companies "wear the same clothes," no two organizations behave in the same manner in the marketplace. In fact, if you were to look more carefully, you would detect that, although companies use the same words or titles, they are in fact organized in very different manners.

The underlying element that determines an organization's structure is the concept of Driving Force, which is at the root of every business strategy.

Take, for example, 3M and Johnson & Johnson, examples used earlier. 3M is organized around "applications" it uncovers from its knowledge of polymer chemistry—its Driving Force. As a result, it has an Abrasive Systems Division, an Aerospace and Aircraft Division, an Electrical Markets Division, an Industrial Adhesives and Tapes Division, a Medical Division, and an Office Supplies Division, to name a few, and all of these divisions refect different applications of 3M's root Driving Force: polymer chemistry. Each division has its own sales, marketing, and manufacturing functions, since these tend to require different skills from one application to another, using different methods to get to market. Some divisions sell direct, some use agents and distributors. Some make end-use products; some make components for other companies' products.

Johnson & Johnson is not organized the way 3M is. Its strategy is "satisfying the health needs of doctors, nurses, patients, and mothers"—a user-class-driven strategy. As such, it is organized around where these four groups are accessed. As a result, it has two divisions: a Hospital Division, since this is where doctors, nurses, and patients are found, and a Consumer Division, which is where mothers are found. Manufacturing is thus centralized, while each division has its own sales and marketing organizations. All the products aimed at doctors, nurses, and patients go through the Hospital Division, and all the products aimed at mothers go through the Consumer Division.

There was a fad in the 1970s and 1980s to reorganize and restructure companies. After the reorganization, the most difficult question to answer became: "Now that we are reorganized, where are we going?"

In our view, *structure follows strategy*. The organization structure of the business must support the direction of that business. We have further learned that each Driving Force requires a slightly different organization structure.

Critical Issues That Relate to Systems and Processes
The next discussion that leads to Critical Issues is one that revolves around the subject of *systems and processes*. Many companies today have purchased sophisticated and costly electronic information systems only to find out some time later that the systems are not supportive of the company's business strategy. Again, our view is that all information systems must be aligned with the direction of the organization and that there are usually issues that surface in the area of systems and processes.

Critical Issues That Relate to Skills and Competencies
When an organization changes its direction, this change will usually require the acquisition of a new set of skills. These skills can be developed, but frequently they do not reside in-house and must be acquired, thus giving rise to another set of Critical Issues.

Critical Issues That Relate to Compensation

In spite of all the titles or power you might think you have over people, experience has convinced us that *people do not do what you want them to do; people do what they are paid to do.* If your strategy says that you want your people to behave in a certain manner but your compensation system rewards them to do something different, at the end of the year they will have done what they were paid to do and not what you wanted them to do.

As a result, another area of discussion that raises Critical Issues is the subject of compensation, to ensure that the compensation of key individuals is geared to supporting the strategy and direction of the business.

To illustrate the significance of identifying the Critical Issues to be resolved to implement the strategy, we refer by way of example to one of our clients. When the Retail Division of First National Bank of South Africa (FNB), a Division of FirstRand Bank Limited, went through the Strategic Thinking Process in 1999, the bank decided that its future strategy would be user class driven, specifically entities that required financial services. The bank would then respond to the needs of this user class with a variety of different financial services to meet those needs.

When management examined two of their Critical Issues, they realized they would be unable to implement the strategy without making significant changes in skills, capabilities, and compensation plans. They had some challenges in these areas, specifically in their 1,000-plus outlets located across the geography of South Africa where their entities needed to be serviced.

To provide services and effectively respond to their customers' needs would require specific marketing and customer service skills when dealing with the customers. Management quickly realized that there was a misalignment. The key skills in the branches were administrative, not marketing and service.

The compensation plans were, as a result, also misaligned and not geared to rewarding good service and sales. They were geared to good administration. In fact, branch managers were promoted to the next senior branch managerial position on the quality of their audit reports.

So just by looking at these two components of Critical Issue identification, FNB realized that it would have to make drastic changes to the skills, capabilities, and compensation plans within their branch network to implement the user-class-driven strategy.

Similarly, gearing the Strategic Thinking Process to examining those four specific areas—structure, systems and processes, skills and competencies, and compensation— will surface a number of Critical Issues, which are then identified and assigned to specific individuals for resolution. The expected results are articulated, the macro action steps are listed, other people that need to be involved are assigned to each team; and completion and review dates are established. These Critical Issues then become "the plan" for the organization, and it is the ongoing management and resolution of these issues that makes the CEO's vision a reality over time. It is how the strategy is deployed successfully.

CRITICAL ISSUES AS FORMING
THE BRIDGE TO STRATEGY DEPLOYMENT

At this point, our clients get to work on the Critical Issues. These are the handful of essential initiatives that form the basis of the new strategy. These Critical Issues are one of the most crucial outputs from the Strategic Thinking Process. They are the keys to successful deployment because they have been chosen and agreed upon by those who will carry out the strategy. Once decided, these issues are assigned to individuals to drive them to conclusion. This is where the rubber hits the road—and where the commitment you have developed among these managers will flesh out the strategy and make it happen.

CLOSING THE LOOP

Figure 5.3 shows how all the concepts presented tie together into a cohesive whole.

The box at the top of Figure 5.3 represents the output of our Strategic Thinking Process. The *strategic profile* is a description of what an organization wants to look like at some point in the future. The inside of the box contains the content of this picture. The Critical Issues make up the bridge that needs to be crossed in order to go from what the company looks like today to what it wants to look like tomorrow. Next comes planning time.

FIGURE 5.3 STRATEGIC PROFILE DETAIL

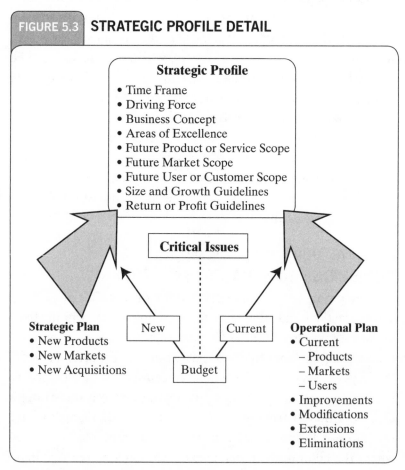

The Operational Plan

The next task is to examine the organization's current activities and decide which products, customers, and markets need to be improved or modified. Moreover, management must identify those that need to be eliminated because they no longer fit the vision of what the company is trying to become.

One of the most difficult decisions we find management having to make, if they do not have what we call a *strategic filter*, is not what to do but rather *what not to do anymore*. This is because there is always someone telling management to "hang in" a little longer with activities that are not productive because they are a poor fit with the strategy—they will turn the corner soon. But in fact, they never do. During the operational planning stage, these decisions become easier to make because all participants have agreed on that strategic filter, and that those activities no longer fit their aspiration of the type of company they are trying to build.

Said Mary Ann Tsao, executive director of DPI client the Tsao Foundation: "With limited resources and so much to do, we must be strategic in our objectives, thorough in our assessments, and targeted in our programming. DPI's Strategic Thinking Process is absolutely priceless. Tsao Foundation has benefited tremendously from it. I highly recommend it!"

The Strategic Plan

In our view, a strategic plan is one that will alter the "look" of an organization in the future. The key elements that will alter the look of a company in the future are the new products, new customers, and new markets that the company wants to add to that look. A plan now needs to be constructed to make these happen.

Our experience shows that if you want to give birth to brand-new activities (products, markets, and acquisitions), it is wise to have people other than those who are running your current businesses "midwife" these projects to birth. The rationale is simple: those running your current businesses have a locomotive on their hands, and keeping that engine on track will require all their time and energy. As such, it is wise to have new activities managed outside the normal structure of the current business.

The Strategic Profile as the Target for All Decisions

As illustrated in Figure 3.10, the strategic profile becomes the target for all the decisions that are made in the organization. Plans and decisions that fit inside the frame of this profile are pursued, and those that do not fit are not.

PHASE 3. SETTING STRATEGIC OBJECTIVES

Strategic objectives are not operational objectives. They do not pertain to functions within a company but rather to a company's future profile, which consists of products, customers, industry segments, and geographic markets. Strategic objectives are the "hills" that we must defend or capture in these four areas that will make our strategy succeed or fail.

This phase consists of a one-day work session, and it is dedicated to the construction of the strategic objectives as well as the plans to achieve the objectives.

PHASE 4. TWO CRITICAL ISSUES MEETINGS

One CEO client said: "You DPI guys are no more than strategic enforcers. Because we scheduled a meeting with you to talk about Critical Issues, we show up. Otherwise, we'd find something else to do. And when we show up, we know what questions you are going to ask. So we work our butts off because no one wants to go to that meeting and report 'no progress.'"

We thought that was a very good way of describing our involvement in the deployment of the strategy as well as in its formulation.

Phase 4 consists of two quarterly, half-day meetings with the CEO and the management team to review progress on the Critical Issues. At these meetings, the "owner" of each issue is expected to give a report of progress. These meetings give the CEO an opportunity to do the following:

- Assess the progress, or nonprogress, on each issue
- Determine whether the issue is on track or off track
- Judge whether the work on each issue is proceeding at the proper pace
- Remove any obstacles into which the owners and their teams are running
- Make any midcourse corrections

PHASE 5. REVIEW AND REVISIT SESSION

Some 10 to 12 months after Phase 2, most clients want to review, or revisit, their previous conclusions. Because these conclusions were based on a certain number of assumptions as to what might or might not occur in the environment, most CEOs want to revisit them to see which proved to be right and which ones wrong. This reassessment allows the client to fine-tune the strategy and occasionally pick up a Critical Issue or two that were missed the first time through the process.

Glen Barton, the CEO at Caterpillar, Inc., from 1999 to 2006, commented on the process:

> We went through a number of consultants who worked with us. Among several others we had the top strategy consultants at the time, Michael Porter and Noel Tichy who had worked with General Electric on their breakout

process. . . . Rather than spending two or three years getting the background that a traditional strategy consultant like Porter might have wanted, we felt the DPI process was a much more straightforward approach that we would be comfortable with and that would get faster results, which at the time was important.

Some of these consulting projects never seem to end. They just keep rolling and rolling and getting bigger and bigger, and longer and longer, and more involved. . . . In the last 10 years we have used DPI's Strategic Thinking Process many times, and when we undertake it, we know there's an end. And when we get to that end, there are decisions we're going to make and directions we're going to take, and we'll move on from that.

CONCLUSION: ANTICIPATING THE IMPLICATIONS OF THE STRATEGY

"Thinking," said Henry Ford, "is a difficult activity. That is why so many people don't practice that habit."

Often, when chief executives change the strategy and direction of their organizations, they do not take the time to think through the implications of those changes. As a result, CEOs end up reacting to the changes as they encounter them.

Every change in strategy—even a minor one—will bring about implications of one kind or another. If you want your strategy to succeed, you must now devote time and thought to identifying the issues that stand in the way of making your strategy work. What are all the changes that need to be addressed in order for the strategy to work?

These changes become what we, at DPI, call *Strategic Critical Issues*. These issues become management's agenda, and each issue is assigned to a specific person who becomes the "owner" of the issue and is held responsible and accountable for getting it resolved. It is the successful management and resolution of these issues over time that will ensure implementation of the strategy.

Laurie Dippenaar, chair, FirstRand Limited South Africa, said this:

> We thought if we went through this process, we would get a common understanding and buy-in into our business philosophy. And it definitely achieved that objective. Obviously, what's affected us more than anything else is the fact that it systematically extracts the thinking and ideas from the executives' heads, rather than imposing the consultant's thinking. I think it almost forces it out of their heads. That obviously leads to the strategy being owned by the company, rather than by the consultant. I'm not just repeating what DPI says. It actually works that way.
>
> One of the most valuable contributions to our thinking from the DPI process is that it provides a filter for the opportunities that you're swamped with. You can easily choose the ones that fit strategically so you don't go chasing hares across the plains.

SUMMARY

Strategic thinking is the most important skill required of a chief executive officer and leader of an organization. Followers generally do not follow leaders blindly, and unless a leader can articulate his or her vision and get the commitment of followers to it, he or she forges ahead alone. In researching the subject of leadership and what some of the most common characteristics of leaders across cultures and organizations were, we found four basic traits that were common and appeared in all transformational leaders, irrespective of organization or country:

1. Leaders have a clear vision for the organization.
2. Leaders have the ability to communicate this vision to others.

3. Leaders have the ability to motivate others to work toward the vision.
4. Leaders have the ability to "work the system" to get things done.

Our experience has shown that leaders have great difficulty articulating their strategy and vision to others. Thus, it becomes imperative for leaders to clearly understand the Strategic Thinking Process in order to involve others in the development of the strategy. This is how motivation, commitment, and successful implementation will result.

Said Chong Siak Ching, the CEO of DPI client Ascendas:

> I think the involvement of the whole senior management team extending a couple of layers down into the organization is essential. We developed a future understanding of the business and the competitive landscape. And also because we run an international organization, it is critical that the HQ and organizations in other countries are aligned with a consistent definition of the strategic direction. So they were all part of the development of the strategy, and they own it. And this makes it much easier to keep everyone on track across the business sectors and countries.
>
> I believe that the discipline with which we conducted the whole Strategic Thinking Process resulted in clarity of the business concept. And when the business strategy is clear, then everything else falls into line. The DPI Strategic Thinking Process ensures that the business concept, people, capabilities, goals, and targets are all in alignment. It is critical that we have that.

Once the strategy skill has been learned and mastered, the next skill that a leader needs to master is that of innovation, which will be described in the following three chapters.

PART 3

THE LEADER
AS INNOVATOR

CHAPTER 6

Innovation: The Fuel of Corporate Longevity

ithout continuous innovation, organizations sputter and die. Nonetheless, most organizations practice innovation in a haphazard manner, apparently hoping that it will happen. In a recent survey we conducted, two-thirds of the respondents said they had no formal program to encourage the search for and development of new products, customers, or markets.

Partly because of this, the United States is losing its innovative prowess. In July 2011 *Forbes* published the list of the world's most innovative companies. Fewer than half of the top 50 companies are American companies. However, the "usual suspects" are very much on the list: Amazon.com, Apple, Procter & Gamble, and PepsiCo. In fact, in these most successful companies, innovation is a paranoiac need. The lifeline of any organization is its ability to continuously find opportunities for new products or services and to develop better processes to manufacture and deliver them.

An American CEO who subscribes to this view is Neil McDonough of FLEXcon. In an interview with DPI's *The Strategist* magazine, he described the impact that DPI's Process of Strategic Innovation has had on his firm:

> New products are the lifeblood of our company. We put this process into place about 18 months ago. And after 18 months, 30 percent of our sales are from new products. We started with a goal of 30 percent in three years. Obviously we blew that away. Through the first 4 months of this year, we have come up with 179 products using combinations of materials we had never made before. We made them and sold them. So this has been very successful for us.

Despite its recognized importance, the majority of organizations fail to innovate successfully, often leading to their subsequent demise. There was a time, not so long ago, that when you went to the national sales meeting, you were treated to a barrage of color slides shown through projectors made by Kodak or Bell + Howell. Then along came PowerPoint, and for better or worse, those ubiquitous projectors, and the slide-making equipment that went with them, were obsolete.

There was a time, not so long ago, when every desk in an office had a Wang word processor, which promised a "paperless office." Then came the PC, and Wang was out of business almost overnight.

There was a time, not so long ago, when Keds were the leading sneakers for kids. Then along came Nike and Reebok.

There was a time, not so long ago, when Nokia was the dominant and most profitable mobile phone maker. Now the company stares out bleakly through the "windows" of their infamous "burning platform."

There was a time, not so long ago, when Creative Technology's ubiquitous Sound Blaster made it the darling of the Singapore technology scene. Now Creative Technology stumbles from one quarterly loss to another, unsuccessfully groping for "the next big thing."

There was a time, not so long ago, when Kodak accounted for 90 percent of photographic film sales in the United States. There was a time, not so long ago, when Kodak invented digital imaging. Now Kodak is bankrupt.

WHY COMPANIES LOSE SUPREMACY

There was a time, not so long ago, when those companies and many more, such as Addressograph, Multigraph, Atari, Polaroid, MG Rover, Borders, Nortel, and Blockbuster Video, were powerhouses in their respective sandboxes. Just a few years later, however, their supremacy had disintegrated together with their stock prices, and billions in shareholder value had been destroyed. What did these companies do, or not do, to descend from the ecstasy of supremacy to the footnotes of corporate history books?

LACK OF STRATEGIC PRODUCT INNOVATION

The strategy of most companies is deployed through the introduction and commercialization of new products. Therefore, any company that wishes to perpetuate its supremacy over a long period of time needs to have in place an ongoing, aggressive, and successful *new product creation program.* Unfortunately, such was not the case in the companies mentioned above. However, many other companies, those that had ongoing new product development programs, could extend their supremacy over their competitors for very long periods of time, companies such as Johnson & Johnson, Caterpillar, 3M, Mercedes, Sony, Honda, and Microsoft.

LACK OF PRODUCTS THAT ARE TRULY NEW

If a leader wishes to change the *strategic profile* of the company—its products, customers, and markets—he or she needs to do so through the creation and commercialization of *new* products. During our research into the subject of product innovation, we noticed that most companies concentrate their entire product innovation effort on incremental or marginal improvements to *existing products*. Our experience with hundreds of clients worldwide is that it is not uncommon for 95 percent of new product development investment to be directed toward incremental improvements on existing products, not new-to-the-market products. This type of product innovation is not strategic in nature since there is no attempt to change the "look" of the products the company offers.

In fact, while working with companies considered to be the best at product innovation, we discovered that even these companies had difficulty defining what a *new product* was. Thus our first area of investigation was to identify the various categories of new product opportunities. Over time, we uncovered *five categories* of new product opportunities:

- *New to the market.* These products, when introduced, were unique to the market and the world. No similar products existed anywhere. Examples are 3M's Post-it notes, Sony's Walkman VCR, and Apple's iPad.
- *New to us.* When Panasonic introduced its own version of the VCR, it was not new to the market because Sony had produced a VCR before, but it was new to Panasonic.
- *Product extensions.* In this category, we find two types: *incremental extensions* and *quantum leap extensions*. An example of an *incremental extension* is 3M's adaptation of the original Post-it notes into larger sizes, shapes, and colors. The adaptations have kept coming and now include flags, tabs, and dispensers. Boeing's announcement of a supersonic passenger jet is a *quantum leap extension*. The technology

required is a significant step beyond making its standard passenger jets.

- **New customers.** This category applies to the introduction of current products to new customers, such as e-readers tapping into the textbook market.
- **New markets.** This category applies to the introduction of current products to new market segments or new geographic areas, such as Subway's steady global expansion.

THE EM-PHÁ-SIS ON THE WRONG SYL-LÁ-BLE

The next area we investigated: In which category did companies invest most of their resources? Guess what over 200 companies answered? Right: *product extensions*—of the *incremental* type. The food and packaged goods industries, for example, have perfected the art of "new-and-improved" products in different colors and sizes. Unfortunately, incremental extensions bring only *incremental revenue increases*. Only *new-to-the-market products* create new revenue streams. Most companies are putting their em-phá-sis on the wrong syl-lá-able. In other words, they are pouring their money into the wrong type of product innovation.

Demonstration of this phenomenon is evident when one examines who it was that introduced "game changer" products into an established industry. Take a look at this list of game changers and ask, "What's the common characteristic?"

- Apple's iPhone
- Tata's Nano car
- Herb Kelleher's Southwest Airlines
- Chad Hurley, Steve Chen, and Jawed Karim's YouTube
- Serious Energy's iWindow

The answer lies not in the game changer itself but in who it was that introduced it. None of these creators was an existing player in the sandbox that the company entered. The companies had nothing to lose by taking a calculated risk. They didn't have the "baggage" of the incumbents. As a result they didn't fall prey to the deadly mindsets that many organizations subconsciously exhibit. To overcome these mindsets, a formal process of innovation is required, and it must be made available to the entire organization.

THE FOUR DEADLY SINS THAT KILL STRATEGIC PRODUCT INNOVATION

Since new-to-the-market products are the essence of strategic supremacy, we then set out to identify the obstacles that caused companies to spend almost all of their time, money, and energy on product extensions at the expense of new-to-the-market products. Our discovery? Most companies committed one or more of four "sins" that kill new product creation and lead to a company's loss of supremacy over its competitors. Unfortunately, all four were self-inflicted wounds.

SIN 1. TOO MUCH FOCUS ON CURRENT CUSTOMERS

Whom do most books on product innovation tell you to consult in order to get inspiration for new products? The obvious answer: your customers. Wrong. Dead wrong! If a company focuses its entire effort on current customers as a source of inspiration for new products, it will always end up with *incremental* products. The reason is very simple. *Current* customers are very good at telling you what is *currently wrong* with your *current product*. They can do this well because they do side-by-side comparisons, and they identify *performance gaps* in your product relative to your competitors. Naturally, you go back to the factory, tweak the product a little, and come back with an incremental improvement. And the pattern is set and keeps repeating itself.

Worse than that, your current customers can begin to *dominate* your product development process. We often see this scenario when we work with clients. Borroughs Corporation, a company that makes, among other things, checkout lanes for retail stores, had gradually gotten itself into this predicament. The company found itself responding to nearly every customer request for tweaks, refinements, and custom designs. Said CEO Tim Tyler: "It was driving our inventories and engineering costs through the roof. I read an article in *Fortune* about Boeing and how it was faced with the problem of having seven or eight airplane frame models, yet it was offering something like 33,000 different variations of galleys and bathrooms, and that was us to a T."

Borroughs used DPI's *Strategic Product Innovation Process* to analyze the problem, and it came up with a game changing solution: a standardized product that meets all its customers' essential needs. That product is also easily customizable to fit each customer's unique "look"—all at a very competitive cost. Customers readily embraced the concept, and Borroughs' margins recovered nicely.

You cannot depend on current customers for your new product ideas because they are not very competent at telling you what they will need *in the future*. The following are some examples.

Not one of 3M's millions of customers ever asked 3M for Post-it notes. Not one of Chrysler's millions of customers ever asked for a minivan. Not one of Sony's millions of customers ever asked Akio Morita, the founder of Sony, for a Discman or a VCR. No one on this planet ever asked Steve Jobs and Steve Wozniak for an Apple computer or an iPod or an iPad. And the list goes on. These are all products that originated in the minds of the creator, not the recipient. There is a very good reason for this, as articulated by Morita in his 1986 autobiography *Made in Japan*: "Our plan is to influence the public with new products instead of asking which products they want. The public doesn't know what is possible. We do."

Another person who said it as eloquently was the former CEO of 3M, Livio DeSimone, who told *Fortune* magazine: "The most interesting products are the ones that people need but can't articulate that they need."

Steve Jobs, perhaps the best and most influential innovator in recent times said: "It's not the customers' job to know what they want."

In order to breed competitive supremacy and create new revenue streams, it is imperative to concentrate a company's product innovation resources on new-to-the-market products.

These are products that satisfy future implicit needs that you have identified and that your customers cannot articulate to you today. In this manner, the result will be products that will allow you to change the game and perpetuate your supremacy.

Not all of us are blessed with the subconscious "nose" of Jobs or Morita. Our ability to "sniff out" future implicit needs of current and future customers may be poor by comparison. Fortunately, if you know where to look, identifying changing needs is not as hard or miraculous as it may seem.

SIN 2. THE PROTECT-THE-CASH-COW MENTALITY

Every company, over time, has products that become cash cows. Never worship at the altar of the cash cow. You will lose your supremacy. IBM is a case in point.

IBM's cash cow, as we all know, had been its mainframes, once the workhorses of the computing industry. In 1968, in its Swiss laboratories, IBM invented the first microchip—the RISC chip—with more processing capacity than its smaller mainframes. A small computer prototype, powered by this chip, was built and could have been the first PC the world saw. IBM, however, made a deliberate decision not to introduce that chip because it could foresee the devastation it might have on its mainframe business. In 1994, 26 years later and maybe 26 years too late, IBM finally introduced the RISC chip under the name PowerPC. In the meantime, IBM lost the opportunity to be the powerhouse in the consumer market that it was in the business market. In 2005, IBM eventually admitted defeat in the PC space and sold out this arm to Lenovo.

The same happened at Xerox. The company worshiped so fervently at the altar of large copiers that it did not see the advent of a Stealth Competitor—Canon—with small copiers. Furthermore, it failed to capitalize on unique inventions that were developed in its Silicon Valley laboratories, such as the mouse and the inkjet printer, both used successfully by Apple later.

General Motors' fixation on large, gas-guzzling cars of questionable quality caused it to fail to foresee the entry of Toyota and Honda into the U.S. market with small, high-quality cars that have reduced GM to half the company it used to be.

A few years back Kodak had a market capitalization in excess of $31 billion, and it was the undisputed king of photographic imaging. Then it invented digital imaging, promptly got cold feet over fears of cannibalizing its chemical-based cash cow, and left its technology on the shelf, leading to its ultimate demise. It is a cruel irony that the remaining value of this once venerable brand is in the 1,100 digital imaging patents it owns yet failed to leverage. According to Olivier Laurent, news editor of the *British Journal of Photography*, in an article published in the *Guardian UK*: "Kodak falls in the 'creative destruction of the digital age.'"

Laurent continues:

> Kodak was the first company to create the digital camera, but back then most of its profits came from selling chemicals [used for developing film], and the company was afraid to invest because they thought it would eat into the traditional business. When they realized the digital market was here to stay, it had overtaken film, and all of Kodak's competitors had far superior digital cameras. Kodak's were never as good, and the company lost its "Kodak moment" reputation as the best in the business.

How the scenario would have played out if Kodak had kept up investment in its own groundbreaking digital technology is left for business schools to ponder.

We are not suggesting that you slaughter your cash cows on a whim. Singapore Airline's cash cow is business-class travelers, and that's not going to change anytime soon. However, savvy competitors will attack your defenses, and sooner or later they will be breached. New technologies can never be put back into Pandora's box. So, if someone is going to destroy your cash cow, it might as well be you.

Neil McDonough, the CEO of long-term DPI client FLEXcon, agrees: "We started talking about ourselves as our own best competitor. Now we offer the best competitive choice, within one house, of short customized runs or standard products."

SIN 3. THE MATURE MARKET SYNDROME

"Our industry is mature. There is no more growth in these markets." Many people would claim that the reason products become generic, prices come down to the lowest levels, and growth stops is that the "market is mature." However, mature markets, in our view, are a myth.

Consider some examples. Who would have thought 15 years ago that people would pay $300 for a pair of shoes? Running shoes at that! After all, everyone had a pair of $10 sneakers, and the market was mature. Then along came Nike and Reebok, and the "mature market" exploded.

Who would have believed a few years ago that anyone would pay $4 for a cup of coffee? Yet Starbucks revolutionized the coffee business by introducing unique products and marketing in a "mature" industry dominated by Dunkin' Donuts for decades. Dunkin' Donuts had mastered the perfect 50-cent "bottomless" cup. A cup of coffee, after all, was just a cup of coffee.

Who would have though 15 years ago that people would pay $5,000 for a bicycle? After all, everyone had a $100 bicycle, and the market was mature. Then along came Shimano, Cannondale, Trek, and others with 18- and 21-speed bicycles and a new type of bike called a "mountain bike," and the "mature market" exploded.

Two CEOs who have based their success on debunking the notion of "mature markets" are Jack Welch, General Electric's famous ex-CEO, and Lawrence Bossidy, formerly the CEO of Allied Signal. Jack Welch preaches that "mature markets are a state of mind," while Bossidy says, "There is no such thing as a mature market. What we need are mature executives who can make markets grow."

A primary mechanism for growing so-called mature markets is *fragmentation*, leveraging Caesar's principle "Divide and conquer." The cosmetics industry is a master of this. There was a time when most women were content with a simple single skin cream. Today, many women would not dream of such a notion. We have eyelid cream, neck cream, lip cream, and creams for all parts of the female form! By swapping out a single universal cream for a plethora of specialized ones, the market was exploded. Having exhausted the female anatomy, in recent years the sights of cosmetic players have shifted to the male, and the explosion continues. Nivea, Kao, and L'Oréal all have lines targeted at the unfairer sex!

SIN 4. THE COMMODITY PRODUCT MINDSET

Acting on the fallacy "We're in the commodity business" is another mistake that can bring down a company's supremacy. This is also a state of mind. Products become commodities when management convinces itself that they are. It's a self-fulfilling prophecy. If you believe your product is a commodity, then so will your customers. If you believe your product is a commodity, then investment in R&D will be cut back to zero and the focus instead will shift to production efficiency, leading to differentiation on price, the very definition of a commodity.

Kevin Surace is a serial entrepreneur, and former InfoTech executive, who established Serious Energy, a supplier of the new iWindow, based on a number of technical innovations to glass, a product that has been around for centuries. He put it this way in an interview to Peter Day on BBC's World Service Global Business program:

> Somehow buildings, which is a $5 trillion worldwide industry, was left to die. Everyone said it's a commodity business. I said it is a commodity business because nobody went there to do anything about it. So they keep making the old [building material] products that they've made for a hundred years, and they've commoditized themselves. I know companies that have not done a single bit of R&D for the last 30 years. It just became overhead. Now, they wouldn't know how to develop a new product. The last person to do so died 30 years ago!

Another example is baking soda, a "commodity" product that has been around since the days of the pharaohs. One day someone placed a small quantity in a refrigerator and noticed that it absorbed odors. Not so long after, we had baking soda deodorant. Then came baking soda toothpaste, and recently, baking soda diapers.

Frank Purdue pioneered the concept of branding chicken, promising more tender, better-tasting chicken. Before Purdue, chicken was chicken, and the only price factors were supply and demand.

Many food and drink manufacturers have leveraged the "cash rich, time poor" and other consumer trends to turn old commodities into high-value items. Take the humble lettuce, which after a simple clean cut and attractive packaging can see its sales value soar. With its superconvenient Nespresso machine, which dispenses fresh expresso coffee at a touch of a button from individually sealed capsules, Nestlé has successfully persuaded millions of consumers to pay around three times the price of regular ground coffee (on a pound-for-pound basis.)

Then there is the "mother" of all commodities—water. Yet, look at what the French did with water. They have mastered the marketing of this mundane commodity by branding it under a variety of names such as Vittel, Evian, and Perrier. Knowing that people were becoming more concerned about the quality of the water they drink, they began to market bottled water at exorbitant prices. This concept was immediately successful even in places where tap water is excellent and essentially free. Through brilliant marketing, they made water "trendy," creating "designer brands," and they charged even more.

Beverage manufacturers have also taken the concept a big step further, adding nutrients to water to create a new category: sports water. One of these even incorporates the "grandmother" of all commodities: oxygen.

GAINING SUPREMACY FROM NEW-TO-THE-MARKET PRODUCTS

Sony, 3M, Canon, Microsoft, Johnson & Johnson, Caterpillar, Schwab, and many others maintain their control of the sandbox not by introducing "me-too" products but rather by focusing their resources on the creation of new-to-the-market products. These have three inherent characteristics that contribute to their gaining supremacy over their competitors:

- *A period of exclusivity.* When you are the only product in the market, you are the only one.
- *Ability to command premium prices.* During this period of exclusivity, you can obtain premium prices, which you can't charge for me-too products, for which every transaction comes down to haggling over price.
- *Ability to build in barriers.* Being first to the market allows you to build in barriers that make it very difficult for competitors

to gain entry into your game. Apple's pursuit of Samsung through patents and other intellectual property is a good example.

After all, that's what supremacy is all about: changing the game and creating the rules to which competitors who wish to play your game must submit.

THE STRATEGIC PRODUCT INNOVATION PROCESS^{SM}

Strategic supremacy is highly dependent on an organization's ability to create and bring to market new products more often and more quickly than its competitors do. We view new product creation as the fuel of corporate longevity. As stated earlier, 3M, Johnson & Johnson, and Samsung introduce hundreds of new products every year. The secret of these product innovator superstars is *a deliberate process* that *causes* product innovation. This systematic process is known and used by everyone in the company.

Observing this phenomenon, we at DPI went on to codify this process being practiced implicitly at these kinds of companies. The result is a unique process called *Strategic Product Innovation*, which makes new product creation a learnable, repeatable process. This process can be used by any organization to create and commercialize new-to-the-market products, which leverage the company's Driving Force and Areas of Excellence, and to generate new revenue streams, which allows the company to grow faster than its competitors.

This conscious, repeatable, business practice consists of the following four steps:

1. *Creation.* Carefully monitor the 10 sources in your business environment, which are listed in the next chapter, from which you can create a broad range of opportunities for new-to-the-market products.

2. *Assessment.* Measure the new product opportunities in terms of costs, benefits, strategic fit, and difficulty of implementation. These criteria will let you know which opportunities should be pursued further—and which should be abandoned.

3. *Development.* Once a commitment is made, try to anticipate the critical factors that will cause the new product to succeed or fail in the marketplace.

4. *Pursuit.* Develop a specific implementation plan that promotes success and avoids failure.

In Chapter 7, we expand on these discrete steps in more detail.

The Process of Strategic Product Innovation

T o be a successful innovator, one of the most important realizations the transformative leader must come to is that the organization needs two management systems: one to run the existing businesses and the second to develop concepts for new products, customers, and markets. Most organizations usually have systems and processes to run the existing businesses, but very few have a formal process to develop new ideas and concepts. At this point, some might say that innovation is a haphazard process that cannot be codified. However, our work has shown that if a person or an organization is good at a particular skill, there is a process being practiced, although it has usually been learned through osmosis or it is instinctive. As long as a skill is being learned only through osmosis, it cannot be made into a repeatable business practice. It is for this reason that innovation happens, or seems to happen, in a haphazard manner in most organizations.

The leader's challenge, then, is to understand the process of Innovative Thinking in order to institutionalize it as a formal activity in the organization and to develop the skill in his or her subordinates.

CHANGE: THE RAW MATERIAL OF INNOVATION

Before he or she can learn the Process of Innovation, the leader must understand the role of change in this process. Change is the raw material of innovation. One cannot have innovation without it. There is a direct linear extrapolation between the amount of change found in an organization's business environment and the amount of innovation that is possible there. The more change, the more room for innovation, and the less change, the less innovation. Innovation thrives on change.

As a consequence, innovative leaders also thrive on change. Innovative leaders do not see change as bad but rather as a constant source of opportunity. The attitude that change is healthy is a key difference between a leader and most followers. Seeing change as healthy and as a constant source of opportunity is a critical mindset that the leader must instill in his or her followers. Change, as the root of innovation, is a fundamental concept of innovation; consequently, assessing changes that affect the organization must be a deliberate process that is both promoted and practiced by its leaders.

THE DIFFERENT FORMS OF INNOVATION

Innovation is a much misunderstood word. To some it means technological breakthroughs, while to others it means something akin to the "big bang" theory of the universe.

For the purpose of outlining a Process of Innovative Thinking, we will attempt to describe the different forms that innovation can take. The first distinction that needs to be made is that between innovation and invention. *Innovation* is the broader concept of continuous improvement, whereas *invention* is one form of innovation. Inventions are usually associated with discoveries—technologies, patents, formulas, and so forth. Inventions can lead to major breakthroughs. There are, however, many other forms of innovation that are more mundane but that, over time, can give an organization a sustainable competitive advantage. We will discuss these other forms in the following paragraphs.

There are two key areas of an organization in which innovation or invention can occur. The first is in the development of new products and/or the improvement of current ones, and it is usually referred to as *product innovation*. The second is in the improvement of the processes that sell, manufacture, deliver, or service the products, and it is usually referred to as *process innovation*, or its related cousin, *business model innovation*.

In each of these two areas, we will build a case to demonstrate that the best leaders do not believe in "big bang" innovation but rather in the more mundane approach of marginal but continuous innovation to the organization's products and processes.

If you believe in the "big bang" approach to innovation—namely, invention—it will be a long time between "bangs." One industry that practices this approach is the pharmaceutical industry, in which a new prescription product comes along every dozen years or so. The lack of recent "bangs" combined with expiring patents and the threat of reputable generics explains the ongoing turmoil in the pharmaceutical industry. Some readers may mistake "big bangs" with the notion of new-to-the-market products. However, they are not the same thing. 3M is a good example of an organization that excels in new-to-the-market product introductions, but these are rarely mind-blowing inventions. Rather, they are the clever application of an existing technology (adhesive), as was the case with the Post-it notes. That said, 3M is savvy enough to leverage its new-to-the-market products through continuous innovation; it had hundreds of different versions of its Post-it notepads within months of producing its original yellow, finger-size format. Each additional version was only a marginal, incremental improvement over the previous one. Nonetheless, it is this ability to continuously innovate that gives 3M an edge over its competitors.

One of the primary tasks of a leader (if the organization is to perpetuate itself) is to install a deliberate process of systematic innovation and provide management mechanisms that ensure its practice on a continuous basis by everyone in the organization.

THE INNOVATIVE THINKING PROCESS

The Innovation Process has four distinct steps: creation, assessment, development, and pursuit (see Figure 7.1):

1. *Creation.* Innovative leaders and organizations know where to look in their environments for changes that can be converted into opportunities for new products, customers, or markets or for ways to improve their processes or business model.
2. *Assessment.* Innovative leaders and organizations know how to assess opportunities against four key criteria in order to rank opportunities in terms of their overall potential.
3. *Development.* Innovative leaders and organizations can anticipate the critical factors that will lead to the success or failure of each opportunity.
4. *Pursuit.* Innovative leaders and organizations can develop an implementation plan that promotes success and avoids failure.

STEP 1. CREATION: 10 AREAS OF OPPORTUNITY

"Where do you find all these new ideas?" we asked several of the most innovative people at many of our client firms.

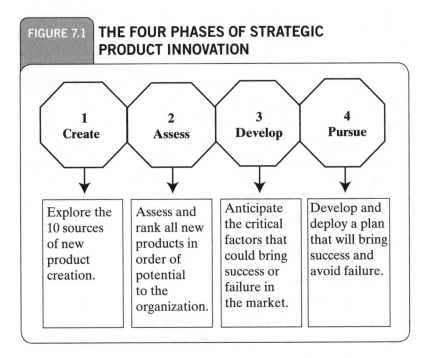

FIGURE 7.1 THE FOUR PHASES OF STRATEGIC PRODUCT INNOVATION

1 Create	2 Assess	3 Develop	4 Pursue
Explore the 10 sources of new product creation.	Assess and rank all new products in order of potential to the organization.	Anticipate the critical factors that could bring success or failure in the market.	Develop and deploy a plan that will bring success and avoid failure.

"Lightning bolts out of the blue," said one. "Gut feeling," said another. "Magic," responded a third person. A fourth said, "It just happened!"

In other words, they did not know and could not attribute a source to their innovation. Interestingly, good innovators frequently cannot describe the process they use, and therefore they attribute the skill to all types of irrelevant occurrences. When we observed these people at work, however, we saw them practicing a very deliberate process that they used over and over but could not describe.

Good innovators know where to look for changes that lend themselves to ideas or concepts for new products or ways to improve the running of the business. There are 10 specific areas of the business that they constantly monitor for changes that can be converted into new opportunities. (Peter Drucker first mentioned several of these changes in his book *Innovation and Entrepreneurship* in 1985.)

1. Unexpected Successes

Every organization has experienced successes that went beyond anyone's wildest dreams. A product sells more briskly than anticipated in Jakarta, Indonesia. Market share goes through the roof in South Africa. Wholesalers to whom the firm had never expected to sell start placing large orders. Unfortunately, in too many organizations unexpected successes are looked on as temporary aberrations that will quickly return to normal. People who see unexpected successes as temporary aberrations will miss out on a number of future opportunities. The right question to ask is, "What caused this success, and how can we spread it out over everything we do?"

2. Unexpected Failures

Every organization has also experienced unexpected miserable failures. In this case most people tend to spend the rest of their careers defending the failures. Instead, they should be asking, "What caused this failure, and how can we turn it into an opportunity the next time?" A dated but striking example to follow is Ford, which was responsible for one of the worst new product introductions ever: the Edsel. However, the automaker was smart enough to learn from this failure, and only a few years later, it introduced the most successful new car to date—the Mustang. It is still in production today, 50 years after the Mustang prototype was launched in 1962.

3. Unexpected External Events

Back in the late 1970s, IBM was merrily following its five-year business plan when Apple introduced the personal computer (PC). To IBM, this was a totally unexpected event. IBM was, therefore, faced with two options: one was to ignore the event, while the second, which it wisely chose, was to "tweak" its business plan a little and introduce a PC of its own, which became the industry leader.

Our guess is that Nokia had no inkling of Apple's entry into the mobile phone sandbox. In a short span of several years, Steve Jobs transformed at least four industries: mobile phones, computing, content distribution, and animation.

The right question in this instance is, "How can we turn this external event into a new product or customer?"

4. Process Weaknesses

All organizations are composed of various processes, procedures, or systems: a sales order entry system, an accounts payable system, a manufacturing process, a distribution system, a quality audit process, a sales refund procedure, an inventory control system, and so forth. Every process or system in existence has one of three things wrong with it:

1. A bottleneck
2. A weak link
3. A missing link

If we spend a little time identifying and describing the various processes that exist in our organization and then ask, "What bottlenecks, weak links, or missing links are there in these processes, and how can we eliminate them?" the query will surely give rise to a number of innovative solutions that will make these processes more effective.

The small island state of Singapore is well known throughout the world for its all-around efficiency, in particular, its government agencies. There is one in particular that we would draw your attention to: the Accounting, Corporate & Regulatory Authority, or ACRA in short. Among the many transactions that one can perform online is probably the fastest and most efficient way to register a business anywhere in the world. Go to www.acra.gov.sg. All it takes is a minute and a valid credit card! One DPI partner likes to recount the time he was in a coffee bar and overheard an interview with a well-known entrepreneur who was asked by the reporter why the company had set up shop in Singapore as opposed to Hong Kong. The reply was that it was easier to incorporate a company in Singapore. Sometimes it really is the small things that make a difference.

5. Structural Changes in the Industry

When the "rules of the game" are suddenly changed in an industry, the changes will usually bring on turmoil, meaning threats for some but opportunities for others. When deregulation first hit the healthcare and transportation industries in the Western world, many firms and executives in these businesses saw only the threats associated with these changes.

We are seeing structural changes in industries all around us today: cloud computing, carbon and "pollution" taxes, and so on. What is already obvious is that social media has changed forever the business models of just about every business on Earth that is connected in shape or form to the Internet. Governments have not been spared either in terms of how they engage their citizenry.

The right question to ask is, "How can we transform these structural changes that are happening in our industry into new products, customers, or markets?"

6. High-Growth Areas

Companies need growth in order to perpetuate themselves. Therefore, they need opportunities that can bring more growth than what might be considered normal. To this end, we should search for changes in the present business or related businesses in which growth is occurring faster than two factors: growth in the gross national product (GNP) or in the population size. These are the areas that will bring opportunities with exceptional growth. Just ask yourself why there are shelves upon shelves of accessories for Apple iPhones and iPads.

The iPhone was launched in June 2007. In January 2011, Apple announced that it had sold over 100 million iPhones worldwide. In the fourth quarter of 2011 alone, Apple sold 37 million iPhones. Go figure the rate of growth! Little wonder the shelves upon shelves of iPhone accessories!

7. Converging Technologies

When two or more technologies start to merge, that convergence is bound to produce turmoil and, as a result, opportunity. The convergence of telecommunication and computer technologies that we have been witnessing for the past few decades has created turmoil, in particular, for telecommunication companies, hardware and software firms, and Internet-related firms, and, in general most businesses worldwide. Rather than attempt to defend themselves against these opportunities, organizations should encourage creating new products and services that exploit these convergences.

So the automobile of the future is not about making a better car per se but about making the "best transportation experience on wheels." Electronic innovations, more than mechanical equipment, are changing today's cars.

8. Demographic Changes

The demographics of an organization's customers are not static: they change with time. As a result, if we attempt to anticipate the demographic changes that will occur in our customer base in the future, we are bound to find opportunity. For example, if we look at the current phenomenon of the aging of America—indeed, the aging of most of the developed world—we should be able to see nothing but opportunities. The "silver" industry is worth hundreds of billions of dollars. As the population grows older, there will be new opportunities resulting from the following needs:

1. Financial counseling advice to manage and reinvest monies coming from individual retirement accounts (IRAs) and other programs

2. Specially tailored travel packages
3. Special fountain-of-youth medicines
4. Counseling services to help younger couples take care of aging parents
5. Special living facilities for elderly people

There are four categories of demographic changes that need to be monitored in an organization's customers:

1. Income
2. Age
3. Education
4. Ethnic or cultural mix

The right question to ask is, "What demographic changes are happening or will happen to our customers in these four areas, and how can we convert these into new opportunities?"

9. Perception Changes

The way in which your customers perceive your products changes with time. If you can anticipate the changes of perception that your customers have or will have vis-à-vis your products, you are bound to find opportunity. For example, the automobile was once perceived strictly as a mode of transport. In the 1960s, however, Ford's Lee Iacocca detected that some people perceived the automobile to be a reflection of their lifestyles, and Ford consequently came out with the Mustang—the first "lifestyle" car. Now there is the BMW for the Yuppies, the Volvo for the safety conscious, and so on. Apparently, Americans' perception of the South Korean cars as a quality and value option has continued to climb. In spite of, or perhaps because of, the economic retrenching that America has been in, waiting lists for South Korean cars such as the Hyundai and Kia have steadily grown. In 2012, the Hyundai Elantra was voted the "Car of the Year" in many markets, including the United States.

The right question to ask is, "What changes are happening in our customers' perceptions of our products, and how can we convert these changes into new opportunities?"

10. New Knowledge

New knowledge means inventions, discoveries, patents, and the like. Obviously discoveries, or new knowledge, will always lead to opportunities in the forms of new products or markets. There are far too many new inventions and discoveries that are already in existence to list in this book, but some notable examples are these:

- Shale gas, an alternative energy source of which America reportedly has 70 years' supply
- Traveling wave nuclear reactors, first proposed in 1950 (!) but recently catching the attention of someone with the resources to commercialize them: Bill Gates
- E-coli biodiesel, where the bacteria convert biomass directly into biodiesel
- Metal foams, with hundreds of applications in aerospace, heat control, orthopedics, and many other areas
- Graphene, a *nano sheet* only one atom thick and set to revolutionize transistors, integrated circuits, solar cells, and so on in the coming years
- Robotics

The note of caution here is that inventions can take a long time to commercialize into profitable products. Fiber optics and lasers were invented in the 1950s, but it has only been in recent years that these technologies have been converted into successful products. History has shown that inventions can take as long as 25 years to become commercially viable. Therefore, while it may be wise to seek innovations in some of the other nine areas first, leaders should not be surprised when disruptive technologies from "old new" inventions suddenly appear in their space.

Observations Regarding the Creation Step

During our work with client organizations, we have made several critical observations regarding how these companies go about finding opportunities.

First, all the organizations with which we have worked to date have been bombarded by changes from all 10 areas simultaneously. Lesson number one in corporate life is that no organization is immune to change. The only constant is change, and any organization that tries to hide or protect itself from it through regulation, legislation, or artificial barriers is doomed to complacency and eventual failure. As much as some people may resent it, innovation is creative destruction of the status quo, something that the best leaders are constantly looking to disrupt.

Second, the best leaders do not wait for these changes to occur before responding. In fact, wherever applicable, they will be the ones to initiate them.

Third, there is a direct relationship between the probability of finding opportunity and its source on the list of 10 search areas. The further down the list you must go to find opportunity, the less likely you will be to succeed. The reason is simple: the further it is down the list, the more difficult the change will be to detect and to convert into a successful opportunity. Nonetheless, this is where we found many organizations looking, at the expense of passing by a host of potential opportunities from the top of the list that were easier to detect and exploit.

Fourth, most organizations that are being bombarded by these 10 types of changes have the tendency to see only the threats associated with them, overlooking the opportunities. It is usually people outside the organization who see the opportunities. An effective leader deals with the threats but demands that the organization and its people translate these changes into opportunities as well. As Peter Drucker wrote, "Resources, to produce results, must be allocated to opportunities rather than to problems" (*Innovation and Entrepreneurship*, 1985).

Last, real leaders do not count solely on home runs or the "big bang" approach to innovation. If they do come across "big bang" ideas, all the better. In the meantime, however, they believe in and practice continuous innovation—a mix of new-to-the-market *and* incremental extension varieties—in every aspect of the business and on the part of everyone in the organization.

STEP 2. ASSESSMENT

As a result of the creation step, we now face a multitude of opportunities. As any good innovator knows, not all opportunities are worth pursuing. The second step of innovation is to assess all the opportunities against certain criteria in order to rank them in terms of their potential to the organization.

The first two criteria are obvious enough: cost and benefit. Each opportunity needs to be assessed in terms of its relative cost versus benefit ratio. In fact, a visual grid (the assessment grid in Figure 7.2) can be used to show where each opportunity falls:

- What is the cost of this opportunity?
- What is the benefit of this opportunity?

The next two assessment criteria are less obvious: those of strategic fit and difficulty of implementation. These two criteria are probably more important than the cost/benefit ratio, but unfortunately, they are almost always overlooked.

How well does this opportunity fit the strategy of the business? This is a key question that is often not asked, but it should be. Experience has shown that organizations that try to innovate outside the strategic framework of the business usually do not succeed. The reason is simple: in order to succeed in its core strategic business, an organization develops skills, structures, and systems that are not usually transferable to opportunities outside this framework. A timeless example was Canon's ill-fated decision to enter the PC business, a domain where

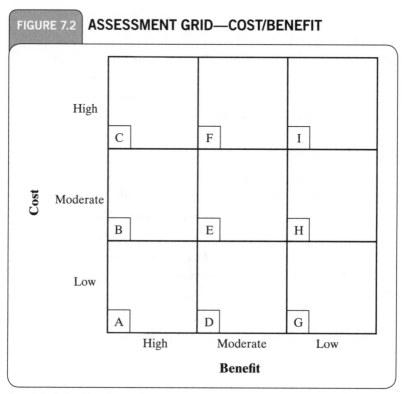

FIGURE 7.2 ASSESSMENT GRID—COST/BENEFIT

Canon's Driving Force of optical technology was of little or no value. This example goes to show the danger of misunderstanding the popular concept of *business adjacencies*. In our view the concept of Driving Force is central to the effective identification of adjacent markets.

The fourth criterion is difficulty of implementation. Again, we have seen many good opportunities fail because management had simply underestimated the degree of difficulty in trying to capitalize on an opportunity. The grid in Figure 7.3 can now be used to assess strategic fit and difficulty of implementation.

Certain conclusions can now be drawn. Obviously, an opportunity that falls in quadrant A in both matrixes is the best we will find—low in cost, high in benefit, good in strategic fit, and

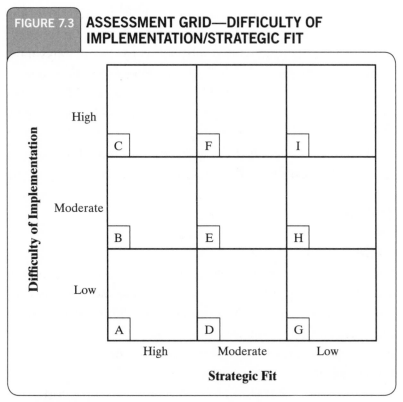

FIGURE 7.3 ASSESSMENT GRID—DIFFICULTY OF IMPLEMENTATION/STRATEGIC FIT

easy to implement. There is none better. Opportunities in adjacent quadrants—B and D—are probable. Quadrant E opportunities are likely to stray from the strategy of the business and bring less benefit. Quadrant C opportunities bring very high costs together with a high difficulty of implementation. The opportunities in quadrants G, H, and I obviously are risky because they violate most of the four criteria.

Presented with such an assessment, the leader of an organization should use it to read the thought processes of his or her subordinates. For example, if an opportunity falls in quadrant F (but something about that opportunity attracts you to it), the grid specifies exactly what must be done to the opportunity before it can be pursued.

First, a way must be found to make it fit the strategy of the business (a move to the left). Second, ways must be found to reduce the costs (one or two moves down). Third, ways must be found to decrease the difficulty of implementation (one or two moves down). If we can affect these three variables, we can move the opportunity to quadrant A, and it will become viable. If not, it should be left where it is.

As a result of applying the assessment grid to all the opportunities, the best ones—like cream—will rise to the top of the list. These are the ones that we now want to take through the final two steps of the Innovation Process.

STEP 3. DEVELOPMENT

Few organizations have in place a formal process to generate and assess new opportunities. Fewer still have the ability to capitalize on these opportunities successfully. This is the reason for the next two steps in the Innovation Process, which concentrate on anticipating the critical elements that will ensure the successful pursuit of good opportunities.

The development step has two phases. Each opportunity, starting with the best one first, is now examined, and best- and worst-case scenarios are constructed using the results we could expect, were we to pursue this opportunity. The questions asked are these:

- If we pursued this opportunity, what are all the best results this opportunity would bring? (Best-case scenario)
- If we pursued this opportunity, what are all the worst results this opportunity would bring? (Worst-case scenario)

At this point, another filter is brought into the process: It is called the *risk/reward analysis*. The risk/reward analysis is a simple scale that looks like the one shown in Figure 7.4.

One can now ask some additional questions of each opportunity:

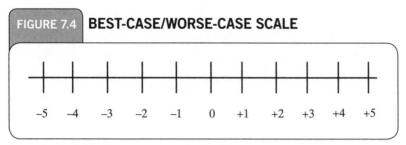

FIGURE 7.4 BEST-CASE/WORSE-CASE SCALE

- Compared to where we are now (the status quo), where will the best-case scenario take us?
- Compared to where we are now (the status quo), where will the worst-case scenario take us?

There are a variety of permutations and combinations that can serve as answers to these two questions. However, here are a few possibilities:

- Best Case: +5; worst case: +1

Conclusion. No risk. Even if we achieve only the worst-case results, we will be better off than we are today.

- Best case: +1; worst case: −5

Conclusion. High risk. There is much more to lose than there is to gain. Is it worth the effort?

- Best case: −1; worst case: −5

Conclusion. How can an opportunity, which is a good thing, take us back from the status quo? Sometimes it happens. A case in point is an opportunity our own firm explored a couple of years ago. One of our competitors, which was three times our size, became available for purchase. Obviously, this was an attractive opportunity since we could have quadrupled our business overnight. However, that particular competitor came with a bad reputation in the marketplace, and we felt that we would acquire not only the competitor but its reputation as well. This, we felt, would set us back from where we were (the status quo). We declined.

- Best case: +3; worst case: −2

Conclusion. If one factor falls on the plus side and the other on the minus side, we must look at the spread between the two. A (+1, −4) is obviously not as good as a (+4, −1).

The result of using risk/reward analysis is that we now can home in on the crème de la crème of opportunities. At the top of our list now are the very best of all the opportunities available.

STEP 4. PURSUIT

The final step of the Innovation Process is to construct an implementation plan that will avoid the worst-case scenario and ensure that the best-case scenario will occur. This step has three phases.

Phase 1 is to take both scenarios (best and worst) from the development step and ask the following questions:

- What critical factors could cause the worst-case scenario?
- What critical factors could cause the best-case scenario?

The critical factors that could cause either scenario are listed by the management team.

The second phase is then to anticipate actions that could prevent the worst-case scenario from occurring and promote the occurrence of the best-case scenario. Both preventive and promotive actions must be aimed at the likely causes since these are critical factors that will bring about either best-case or worst-case results.

The third and final phase of the process is to construct a plan to pursue each opportunity that is still on the list. The plan is a breakdown of the implementation steps or activities needed to implement each opportunity. In the plan, we should include both the promotable and preventive actions identified above. The inclusion of these will ensure that the worst-case results will be avoided and the best-case results achieved.

The process described in this chapter can make innovation happen on a continuous basis. The leader's role is to provide a forum and a framework within which it can occur. This means conducting meetings (forums) in which part of the agenda is dedicated to searching for opportunities together with a formal process (framework) that makes it happen.

John Gardner, in his 1963 book *Self-Renewal*, said that to have renewal, you need the seemingly exclusive conditions of stability and innovation because stability without innovation is stagnation, while innovation without stability is anarchy. He argued that you need to have innovation in content and stability in process, and we concur.

Niccolo Machiavelli once described the innovative person in this way: "The innovator makes enemies of all those who prospered under the old order, and only lukewarm support is forthcoming from those who would prosper under the new." Since we view innovation as "creative destruction" of the status quo, it is easy to understand why people who benefit from the status quo are threatened by it. However, there is no other alternative to progress. Change can be made less threatening to people if it is accompanied by a conscious and visible process.

Steve Jobs said, "Innovation is what distinguishes a leader from a follower," and he managed to influence and inspire the entire Apple organization.

So the next question for the transformative leader becomes, "How can I deploy the proven innovation processes throughout my entire organization?" Turn the page to discover the answer.

CHAPTER 8

Making New Product Creation a Repeatable Business Practice

The message for the transformative leader about effective new product creation is simple: innovation can and must be practiced as a repeatable process. Yet even in the most successful companies such a process is usually not practiced consciously and repeatably. Our 35 years of business experience has convinced us that unless an activity is in the form of a describable process, it will not be consistently practiced, nor will it be transferred as an organizational skill to others.

Moreover, product innovation is an offensive weapon much more than a defensive one. Truly innovative products are by far the best weapons in corporate warfare. Yet one great product alone does not produce long-term success. Product innovation must be done continuously. Think of Pet Rocks, Rubik's Cubes, Cabbage Patch Kids—like the pop charts, commercial history is full of "one-hit wonders," yet most of their names are quickly forgotten after that first "big bang."

Henry Ford, one of the great product innovators, said in his biography entitled *My Life and Work*, "It could almost be written down as a formula that when a man begins to think that he at last has found the method, he had better begin a most searching examination of himself to see whether some part of his brain has not gone to sleep." Product creation, in other words, needs to be a constant process. Too many organizations "go to sleep" after one or two "hits."

As we have said, the key to success is to have a deliberate process of innovation. In the sections that follow, we first outline how DPI clients utilize our Innovation Process as project streams within a formal *innovation project*. Second, we explain how others take steps to make innovation part of the fabric of their culture. Both are required to make innovation a continuous and repeatable business practice.

INNOVATION AS A PART OF THE FABRIC OF THE ORGANIZATION

The following are some useful techniques for making innovative thinking and new product creation a repeatable business practice.

BAN THE WORD *NO*

In the work we do with our clients, we frequently come across middle managers who tell us: "The problem around here is not that we lack new product opportunities. The problem is simply that management turns everything down." In other words, management says no to everything that is proposed as a new product concept. The message that goes out to the organization is that management is not interested in new product opportunities, and the result is that middle management stops proposing them.

Upon a more careful analysis of this phenomenon, we have come to two interesting conclusions. First, we have not met any CEOs or management teams that deliberately attempt to discourage new product creation. We have also noticed that when presented with new opportunities, many of them immediately detect serious flaws in the ideas or their implementation plans and have no choice but to say no. The reason is simple. Management, through the use of very acute questions, can quickly pick the recommendation full of holes, often not because of the product itself but because its implementation plan has not been thought out and is not likely to succeed. The proposal then gets rejected or sent back for more work. This frequently happens because the proposers have not thought through the consequences, risks, or potential problems of their new concept. In other words, they have not considered the development or the pursuit step of the process described in this book. No wonder management says no.

INDOCTRINATE ALL KEY PEOPLE IN THE CONCEPTS AND PROCESSES OF NEW PRODUCT INNOVATION

As mentioned in Chapter 2, during peacetime an army needs few leaders. However, during a time of war, it needs many. The same is true of new product innovation. When there is no competition, there is no apparent need for new product innovators. With intense competition, however, a company needs as many as it can find. Some companies attempt to delegate the development of new concepts to a small group of specialists or experts, mandating them to generate new product opportunities on behalf of the corporation. What these executives fail to realize is that creativity has no geography. All of the people involved in the new product creation "chain," including customers and suppliers, need to be indoctrinated in the concepts. New product creation needs to be delegated widely throughout an organization, not restricted to a small band of specialists.

The best leaders, in our view, can pass on, or teach, their skills to others. As previously mentioned and as demonstrated by the athletics analogy in Chapter 2, we cannot do this until we are fully conscious of the process or methods we use to achieve success.

But the Process of Innovative Thinking can be studied and learned. To win against innovative competition, a company must master the process to a much higher degree than its competitors.

DEVELOP A SYSTEM TO COLLECT NEW PRODUCT CONCEPTS

One of the most important realizations management must come to is that any organization needs two management systems. One is used to run the existing business, and the second is used to run the future business. The first is dedicated to the management of current products, current customers, and current markets. The second is dedicated to the development of concepts for future products, future customers, and future markets. The two systems are different and need to be kept separate. The first is usually past oriented and deals with problems and difficulties that current products are encountering in current markets. The second needs to be future oriented, and it needs to deal with the creation of future products for future markets.

Most organizations have sophisticated systems and formal forums and meetings to run the current business, but few have a formal process to create new product ideas and concepts. Managers are generally presented with problems, and they see their role as resolvers of problems. If that is their central identity and their basis for recognition, the chances are that they, and the organization, will never be very innovative. Reports that are produced in most organizations have a tendency to focus on negative deviations and underperformance. Such systems tend to breed problem solvers and not opportunity generators. Management vision therefore needs to be focused on opportunity and to be future oriented. Opportunity creation, selection, and pursuit must be supported by formal structures and systems and managed apart from what's broken at this moment, or from responding to competitive pressures—all activities that breed reactive behavior. In our view, the transformational leader is one that keeps one eye each on problems and opportunities.

Innovative thinking needs to breed proactive behavior. Management meetings, therefore, should have separate agendas that focus on opportunities as well as problems. Management's challenge, then, is to understand the process of new product creation and innovative thinking in order to institutionalize them as formal activities in the organization.

FORM A NEW PRODUCT COMMITTEE

One way to encourage the development of new product concepts is to have a standing committee that serves as a focal point to review and activate new concepts. Its mandate is not to be the generator of new product concepts but rather the assessor, approver, initiator, and monitor of new opportunities.

ENCOURAGE RISK TAKING

Many a wise manager has remarked: "If you're not making mistakes, you're not making decisions." Companies that live by such a motto have a culture that encourages risk taking. 3M is a case in point. "Make a lot of little mistakes, but try to avoid big ones" is 3M's way of putting it. 3M further encourages risk taking through a concept it calls *bootlegging*. People at 3M are allowed to dedicate 15 percent of their time to any project they wish without the approval of any of their superiors. Google's concept of *innovation time off* is similar to 3M's. Other organizations, notably Lockheed Martin and Boeing, take a different tack by invoking specific *skunkworks teams*. Whatever the approach, innovative thinking involves risk taking—prudent and calculated risk taking, but nevertheless risk taking. None of these organizations, however, bets the house on one roll of the dice.

For example, most people would consider Bell Laboratories to have been one of the more conservative and prudent organizations that ever existed. Yet for over 90 years in the 1900s, from the design of the automatic telephone switchboard, to the development of the transistor, to the invention of semiconductors, to the development of optical fiber cables, Bell produced a continuous stream of innovative winners. Obviously, Bell Labs had a process to assess relative risk versus potential benefit, and that process was endorsed by management. As obvious is the fact that since the breakup of AT&T, under the aegis of Lucent, that process has been shelved.

In many companies, certain management systems discourage risk taking, preferring instead to maximize short-term performance. As recently reported by Adam Davidson in the *New York Times*, in his article *"Will China Outsmart the U.S.?,"* such systems are now pervasive at the top:

> And that's the real problem. From a CEO's perspective, long-term R&D is a lousy investment. The projects cost a lot of money and often fail. And even when they work, some other company can come along and copy all the best ideas free. Charles Holliday, Jr., the CEO of DuPont who retired three years ago, told me that it's tough to get investors to think more than two years ahead—at most. "The stock market pays you for what you can do now," he said. As a result, DuPont isn't the only American company changing the way it does R&D. Corporate research labs at IBM, AT&T, Xerox, and others have also been slimmed way down or cut altogether.

Various ideas to solve this dilemma are being pondered by governance experts. Davidson went on to say:

> The government can't simply pass a law forcing companies to think longer-term, of course. But Congress can do other

things, like shift incentives away from rampant short-termism. It could, for example, reduce capital-gains taxes on stocks held for many years. Alternatively, companies could create different classes of stock, giving more voting rights to those who hold the stocks longer. Another idea popular among businesspeople: enticing foreign PhD students to develop their new ideas in the United States.

The result of short-termism is lower innovative activity and declining competitiveness. The risk-avoidance style of management in existence today in many U.S. companies has already cost the country dearly. This is not a new phenomenon. Step back a few decades and you can discover many inventions that were birthed in the United States but saw the light of day as innovative new products abroad, most notably from Japan.

One example is the transistor, which was invented by Bell Laboratories but exploited by Sony. A second is the video-cassette, which was invented by California-based Ampex but exploited by Sony and Panasonic. The same is happening today, but it is likely to be the Chinese that prosper. In the same article for the *New York Times*, Davidson argued that China is on the verge of leapfrogging the United States in many areas of new invention: "China already has plans to focus on exciting but vague ideas now—like green energy and bio- and nanotechnology—that will most likely become products in the 2020s."

When it comes, product commercialization of these technologies is likely to be accompanied by global shifts in competitiveness. A transition of China from "manufacturer for the world" to "inventor for the world" would have profound impacts on all.

ENCOURAGE SMALL AS WELL AS LARGE PRODUCT INNOVATIONS

The message here is clear. Don't bet the future of the company on the ever elusive "eureka" project. The key is to have a hopper full of new product concepts that can be opened at a moment's notice to allow another new concept to come to life.

MEASURE INNOVATION

As Peter Drucker has said, "If something is important to the organization, measure it!" We couldn't agree more. As previously mentioned, 3M popularized a simple yet profound measure of innovation: it mandates that every one of its 52 divisions produce 25 percent of its revenues from the introduction of new products within the last five years. Rubbermaid does it as well. In fact, Rubbermaid pushes the envelope a bit further, stipulating that 33 percent of revenues come from products newer than five years old and that 25 percent of total revenues be from new markets outside the United States.

A key thing to note about these metrics is that they measure the *outputs* of innovation, not the *Process* of Innovation. When Jim McNerny lost out to Jeff Immelt in the battle to replace Jack Welch as chair and CEO of GE, he made his way to 3M. Subsequently, using the efficiency program GE had adopted as a standard management practice in the 1990s, McNerny tried to "Six Sigmatize" 3M's innovation culture and process. The result? Short-term cost reduction and profit increases at the expense of innovation, followed by reduction in new revenues stream from new products. Today, McNerney is the highly respected CEO of Boeing, an organization much better suited to such a management style.

Moral of the story: measure, yes, but measure the right thing!

REWARD AND COMPENSATE INNOVATION

Again, it is important to recognize that people do not do what you want them to do, but rather, they do what you pay them to do! Therefore, if your people are not rewarded and compensated for their new product creation efforts, these efforts will not occur. Therefore, a must of any new product creation program is that there be in place a visible system of rewards and compensation.

Depending on the strategic thrust of the company, the reward system may need to be skewed to encourage different categories of innovation. If survival is based on staying ahead of the pack, then new-to-the-market innovation may need to be compensated more than product extensions. If the strategy is to be a quick follower, then new-to-us innovation should be better rewarded. The key is that the compensation system of the corporation needs to encourage product innovation that supports the strategy of the business.

TEST NEW PRODUCT INNOVATION OPPORTUNITIES RIGOROUSLY

Product innovation should be encouraged and rewarded but subject to the same disciplines and audits as any other request for funds and resources. Most companies test the justification of capital expenditure requests quite rigorously, but when it comes to doing the same for new product opportunities, they don't quite know where to begin.

The following is a list of questions that can be asked of those presenting a new opportunity to the organization:

New Opportunity Assessment Questions

- What is the source of this opportunity?
- How many other opportunities were considered?
- How did it rank in terms of costs and benefits? Strategic fit and difficulty of implementation?
- How did it rank in terms of risk and reward?
- What is the spread of risk to reward for this opportunitiy versus other opportunities?
- What are the critical factors that will cause success? Failure?
- How will you promote success? Avoid failure?
- What is your implementation plan?
- What do you think is the probability of success of your plan?
- Who will manage the plan?

Those questions are the ones that the presenter and conceiver must ask of his or her own opportunity; and they are the questions that management must responsibly ask and have answered to intelligently evaluate innovative opportunities. Since innovation is manageable, it should be subject to review and objective measurement, and the process is as important as the content.

TURNING PRODUCT INNOVATION INTO A REFLEX

This conscious management process needs to be institutionalized to become a repeatable business practice. In other words, over time the process should become a reflex. The notion of cascading these processes down the organization is also critical to the success of the organization.

The reason is simple: contrary to what many think, it is the processes that management puts into place in the organization that will get people to behave in a certain manner. The dissemination of these fundamental thinking processes throughout the organization is then vital to its success. Unfortunately, thinking is an increasingly rare skill in business today. Yet, the best companies have mastered the skills of innovative thinking, and they have the ability to instill these skills in dozens, hundreds, or even thousands of people throughout the organization.

A SIX-PHASE INNOVATION PROJECT

The following is a brief project overview of the phases in a DPI-led strategic product Innovation Process.

PHASE 1. BRIEFING
First we bring together a diverse mix of participants. We have found that rather than limiting the assignment to product

development specialists, it is essential to involve a selected blend of experienced marketers, sales staff, back office staff, and other seasoned personnel in order to gain a wider perspective.

As many of the participants may be new to the notion of product innovation, they are introduced to the process and the possible mindsets that they need to put aside.

Participants are then guided through the DPI Strategic Innovation Input Survey to which each responds individually. The input from this survey becomes the "raw material" of the process.

PHASE 2. DATA VALIDATION

A DPI facilitator consolidates and assesses the quality of the input from the participants. If necessary, additional steps are taken to ensure a suitable standard of input prior to the workshop at Phase 3.

PHASE 3. TWO-DAY CREATE AND ASSESS WORKSHOP

During this workshop, the process facilitator guides the participants through the first two steps of the Innovation Process. The primary outcome is a list of seemingly plausible product concepts (not ideas!) that have been through an initial first-cut assessment. In addition, there are often many other concepts that are channeled into the "hopper" for future assessment.

PHASE 4. MARKET VALIDATION
AND MANAGEMENT PRESENTATION

Working off-site, teams validate the concepts with more rigor than is possible during a two-day workshop.

The best-validated ideas are then presented to management for review. The crème de la crème are then prepped for Phase 5.

PHASE 5. COMMERCIALIZATION OF THE PLANS

This two-day workshop focuses on the *develop* and *pursue* steps of the process, as discussed in Chapter 7. The result is a set of robust, loaded-for-success commercialization plans.

PHASE 6. GO/NO GO DECISIONS

This final phase is when management makes the necessary go/no go decisions. A concept selected as a "go" is ready for immediate implementation.

SUMMARY

The process described in this book can make new product innovation happen on a continuous basis. The leader's role is to provide a forum and a framework within which it can occur. This means conducting meetings (forums) in which part of the agenda is dedicated to searching for opportunities together with a formal process (framework) that makes it happen.

John Burgess, when he was CEO of U.S. optical equipment manufacturer Reichert, made this process an integral part of his strategy.

Said Burgess in an interview in *The Strategist*:

> We said, "Okay, we've got sort of a product development process in place, but it's slow, and it doesn't have a method for deciding the important questions: *what* products should we develop, and *why*, and what's the *priority*? We were looking for a way to generate new ideas and get the products up and moving, but to be sure that they were needed by the market, doable from our standpoint, and innovative so that we could reestablish our leadership in the market we had decided to go after.
>
> We liked DPI's concepts of the "product hopper" and keeping it full, keeping the product concepts moving, being able to move them from the hopper down through strategic development, and through the *strategic filter*.

The end result: products that would "fit" their market and strategy:

I have a diagram on my wall that I call the "Status of the Strategic Process." I've got a big funnel, my hopper, and a list of products going into it. At the bottom of the funnel is "Opportunity Development." This is a shorter list of products that we are in the process of trying to understand, so that when they get to the strategic filter, we can answer all the questions.

Then there's a line—that's the strategic filter. If they get past that, they go to what we call "Technology Validation." These are products that have gone through the filter but that we are uncertain we have the technology understood to the point where we can move forward with them. We have to be sure they will work.

The next gate is "Proof of Technology." Once we've proven the technology, it goes into the "Product Development Cycle." We have a list of products in there. Then the next gate is "Product Launch." And the last gate is "Production Release"—these products have gone through the process and are now in production.

PART 4

THE LEADER AS SITUATION MANAGER

CHAPTER 9

Balancing Operations and Execution

O nce a strategy is in place and innovative opportunities have been targeted, a leader is left with the task of running the business on a day-to-day basis. All kinds of operational situations will surface while he or she is trying to keep the locomotive on track, demanding yet another set of mental skills as part of the leader's arsenal. What is now required is a framework for operational decision making that leads to the resolution of day-to-day concerns in a manner that continuously edges the organization toward its new strategic profile.

At this point, we are often asked to explain the difference between execution and operations. Our answer is that they are not different. The largest single impediment to the successful balance between operations and strategy execution is the belief that somehow the two things are entirely separate. While it is true that a small number of focused execution teams may be required, the successful execution of a strategy cannot be divorced from the humdrum of day-to-day operations. That is, operations and execution are one and the same thing.

Yet browsing in a bookstore would yield a slew of recent management literature on execution or deployment, a management topic that has become a science all its own.

How did we arrive at a point where management doctrine has established execution as a separate art, and one that is entirely separate from strategy itself and from day-to-day operations?

IT'S THE EXECUTION, STUPID!

History is littered with stories of "brilliant" strategies that never got implemented, such as these:

- HP's planned acquisition of PwC Consulting that would have enabled it to fight mano-a-mano against IBM (who ironically pulled off the purchase itself)
- Motorola's $5 billion bet on the satellite phone, known as Iridium
- Cisco System's $300 million write-off of the once-so-cool Flip video camera
- Royal Bank of Scotland's disastrous determination to acquire ABN AMRO
- Early dot-com darling Pets.com

On paper, these and other failures looked like winners, at least to those that conceived them. These examples also give unfortunate credence to the saying "A strategy is only as good as the paper it is written on."

Modern management thinking places the blame for failed strategies purely on execution. This dramatic simplification of the matter is popular among certain leadership teams, and the consulting firms who "advised" them, who are more than happy to deflect attention away from themselves. "It was a great strategy; unfortunately, it wasn't implemented successfully," they will say, with no sense of irony as to how a strategy can be "great" if it can't be executed!

The result of strategy "execution failures" has been to further separate strategy formulation and its execution, attempting to turn execution into a separate discipline. It is not unusual to see outside consultants being responsible for creating the strategy that in-house people are expected to execute. Implicit acceptance of this practice has led to a host of elaborate "execution systems" that attempt to address the failings of the doctrine itself! A vicious cycle perpetuates.

CHOICELESS DOERS VERSUS THE CHOICE CASCADE

A popular approach to drive execution is to put everything into excruciatingly codified business practices, often in ways that remove the freedom of frontline staff to think for themselves. Inherent in such an approach is a belief that frontline staff cannot be trusted to make decisions!

In the immortal line "I'm sorry, there's nothing I can do; it's company policy" lies the pitfalls of attempting to codify the behavior of the entire workforce at the expense of encouraging critical thinking. To do so is to ignore the intelligence and capabilities manifestly residing within your people. Genetic engineering may be popular in medicine, but if you believe that people are your most important asset, why then would you attempt to remove their genes and insert a management engineered "rule book" instead?

In "The Execution Trap," an article published in the *Harvard Business Review*, Roger Martin describes this phenomenon in an alarmingly crude yet unnervingly accurate parallel—the brain-body analogy. Just as our brain makes the choice to eat an apple and the arms and legs "choicelessly" comply with the resultant instructions, Martin argues that modern management doctrine sees leadership as the brain and the workers as *choiceless doers*.

The alternative, Martin argues, is to see strategy and its execution as a *choice cascade*. Using the analogy of a white-water river, Martin explains:

> To fix our problem with strategy failure, we need to stop thinking in terms of the brain-to-body metaphor. Instead, we should conceive the organization as a white-water river in which choices cascade from the top to the bottom. Each set of rapids is a point in the corporation where choices could be made, with each upstream choice affecting the choice immediately downstream. Those at the top of the company make the broader, more abstract choices involving larger, long-term investments, whereas the employees toward the bottom make more concrete, day-to-day decisions that directly influence customer service and satisfaction.

Hidden in this cascade is the notion that staff members at all levels need to understand the essence of the strategy and be equipped to make good lower-level, often operational, decisions that are in tune with it. For example, top management would debate choices such as "In which sandbox should we participate?" or "How will we win in the chosen sandbox?" These are choices that are dealt with by the Strategic Thinking Process. However, as the cascade flows down the organization, the nature of the choices will begin to change, requiring a different set of critical thinking skills. For example, section managers may ask, "What does the strategy mean for my hiring, training, and employment practices?" A service executive will ask even sharper questions, such as, "What does all this mean to this customer standing in front of me at this very moment?"

Martin makes the final point that "the choice-cascade model isn't nearly as pervasive as the strategy execution model." Perhaps this is because executives implicitly dislike the lack of control inherent in a choice cascade, or perhaps they think it is simply too difficult to develop a culture of critical thinking. Or is it because it feels safer to view frontline staff as choiceless doers who are told exactly what to do and when, how, and under what circumstances to do it—while measuring every aspect of their performance and watching over them at every turn?

We would argue that it is impossible to design an instruction manual to cover every eventuality. We would argue that the missing yet readily available ingredient is a separate set of thinking skills specifically designed to resolve operational decisions.

THE CHOICE CASCADE
AND DECISION MAKING

Solid translation of strategy into day-to-day behavior rests on having great decision makers at all levels. Rather than breed choiceless doers, leaders should foster a decision-making culture. Clearly, this will test the decision-making mettle of those involved, including the leaders. Unfortunately, not all staff members are good decision makers, and those that are may not be able to impart their skills to others because they are not cognizant of their skills.

One key skill that is often lacking is the ability to translate the strategy into an actionable concept that all staff members can understand and then use as a guide into the decisions they make. It is the role of leadership at various levels to aid in this translation for the next level below them. Some organizations have perfected the art, and their performance is commensurate with their strengths. A good example is AirAsia, the leading low-cost carrier in Asia. Their tagline "Now everyone can fly" can be easily translated for any operational staff member. For the in-flight crew, it means that the majority of travelers will be first-time flyers who will require additional support. For the engineers, it implies affordability and a need to judiciously manage costs to keep prices low.

While it is tempting to turn staff members into choice-less robots by developing a rule book for everything, a better approach is to provide the organization with the ability to make consistent, rational decisions that are aligned with the strategy crafted.

Before we are accused of encouraging corporate anarchy, and for reasons of consistent scalability, we are not suggesting that key business processes be consigned to the dustbin. But neither should they remove the ability for sensible staff to think on their feet when it is needed. Unless, of course, you are happy to hear the line "I'm sorry, there's nothing I can do; it's company policy" coming from your own organization.

What is needed is a balance between control and empowered day-to-day decision making. Empowered decision making requires your people to make the right decisions. It's not an understatement to say that the future of any organization is the "summation" of the way staff members at all levels make and implement decisions in response to the situations that confront them on a daily basis. Since business processes can never cover every eventuality, and because not all operating procedures are right at first, a culture of critical thought is required.

In the following chapter we elaborate on our proven decision-making framework, what we refer to as *Situation Management*.

A typical reaction may be, "We don't need a process to make day-to-day decisions." We disagree.

WHY THE NEED FOR A CRITICAL THINKING FRAMEWORK?

Staff members at all levels are confronted with operational challenges such as these:

- An ever increasing number of complex situations within a continually decreasing time frame

- Apparently straightforward issues "bouncing back" to haunt them
- Ensuring that activities support broader yet ambiguous corporate objectives
- The lack of a common approach to resolving common situations
- The expectation that they deliver results in an area new to them and in which they have limited experience and expertise
- Inability to convince management, customers, or partners of the rationale behind the recommendations they make

Most people are required to think about and resolve operational situations on a daily basis, and most do a good job. Why, then, is there a need for a critical thinking framework? The answer is simple: addressing situations is getting more difficult.

Several changes are occurring in business that increase the difficulty of "good thinking" and its associated behaviors. Let's explore four of these changes.

CHANGE 1. THE INFORMATION EXPLOSION

We are in the midst of an information explosion. Although this phenomenon is often cited, the extent of this explosion is not always understood. Researchers have shown that from 1750 to 1900, within a span of *just 150 years*, the amount of information in the world *doubled*. It *doubled* again from 1900 to 1950. It *doubled* again in the 1950s and the 1960s, *tripled* in the 1970s, increased *sevenfold* in the 1980s, and much more in the 1990s and the "noughties."

It has been often quoted that people living in the early 1600s—when Shakespeare was at his prime—received the same amount of information in their entire lifetime as is contained in a single edition of the *New York Times*. If that sounds scary, consider again the research from Richard Alleyne, of the *Daily Telegraph* in his article "Welcome to the Information Age—174 Newspapers a Day": "If you think that you are suffering from information overload, then you may be right—a new study shows everyone is bombarded by the equivalent of 174 newspapers of data a day."

Retrieving, collecting, and organizing data are harder tasks than ever before. Separating relevant from irrelevant information is more and more difficult. Establishing clarity in the midst of this information overload has never been more challenging, and this difficulty increases the risk in our actions. Fast, insightful, and repeatable critical thinking is required for leaders to process this slew of information in an effective manner. It can be argued with some conviction that leaders are "information processors," and as information explodes, suitable thinking processes are required to keep up.

CHANGE 2. THE OBSOLESCENCE OF KNOWLEDGE

The rate at which new technology is replacing old technology is increasing every day. The Massachusetts Institute of Technology has found that one year after graduation, 50 percent of what an engineer learned in school is obsolete. With the increased use of high technology, evolution is almost a daily occurrence. We can no longer depend purely on our own experience and expertise to address situations. More than ever we are asked to resolve situations for which we have little or no firsthand knowledge. When dealing with such situations, we cannot rely on "gut feelings" or intuition.

CHANGE 3. TIME PRESSURES

The consequences of mismanagement are far greater. Mistakes cost far more today than in the past, yet paradoxically we have less time to think due to the increased pace of business. Thinking fast and effectively requires a navigational "map."

CHANGE 4. PEOPLE'S INCREASING NEEDS FOR INCLUSION AND PARTICIPATION

The last change is a social one. More people want to participate in the "thinking" process as ownership has widened substantially. Interested parties want their inputs included, their objectives considered, and their options debated. Thus, there is a need for a common process of Situation Management that each participant involved can understand.

To address these four factors, leaders need to be *conscious* of the *thinking processes* used to address situations.

Unfortunately, even good thinkers are not aware of *how* they think. They are not conscious of the approach, method, or logic that they use to arrive at conclusions. They attribute their ability to "experience-based intuition" or even "gut feel."

This lack of awareness means that they can neither improve their own competence nor help their colleagues or subordinates to improve their skills.

We need to become better thinkers in order to reduce the degree of difficulty in managing situations. And to become better thinkers, we must have a conscious awareness of our process. That is, we need to know *how* we think.

CRITICAL THINKING PROCESSES FOR SITUATION MANAGEMENT

With conscious awareness, leaders will be able to improve these skills and thus the quality of their response to challenging situations. Further, it's only when we are consciously aware of how we think that we can improve our ability as leaders to coach those around us. This is why DPI developed a set of critical thinking processes called *Situation Management.*

Said William Leong, a senior manager at ASE Asia Pacific: "Situation Management provides a fast and systematic way to resolve problems in today's highly competitive environment. It enables seasoned managers to map their lifelong knowledge, experience, and know-how to a simple framework for efficient troubleshooting and forms a practical mentoring and coaching tool for subordinates."

At the heart of Situation Management are four rational processes: first, identifying and establishing clarity around the priority issues; second, analyzing the issues to get to the "heart of the problem"; third, choosing the right course of action; and finally, planning and implementing the chosen actions.

Theresa Lim, a director from Avago Technologies (Singapore), believes that Situation Management Processes provide the operational thinking tools to achieve this: "Its proven critical thinking framework, combined with DPI's practical, real-world philosophy, makes Situation Management a must for all managers."

In the next chapter, we will look critically at what is involved in effective Situation Management. How exactly does one set about the task of identifying priority issues? How does one analyze a problem? And how does this process differ from choosing the right course of action? Finally, what is involved in the effective planning and implementing of that action?

CHAPTER 10

The Situation Management Framework

F rom the moment people enter their offices each morning, or if they have the (mis)fortune of having smartphones, on a 24/7 basis, they are constantly bombarded with a variety of issues that are communicated to them through any one of many devices:

- Mail
- E-mail
- Twitter
- Phone calls
- Reports
- Faxes
- Phone messages
- Meeting notices

This is true of chief executives, presidents, general managers, middle managers, secretaries, supervisors, operators, and even janitors. Therefore, these people need to possess a running inventory of these various issues in order to come up with a list of things to do immediately, another set of items that should be immediately delegated to others, and a final set that can be placed on the back burner. In other words, they need to place the issues in order of priority. Some do it mentally, while others do it visually—on paper, or in a personal organizer of some sort.

As they work down the list, guess what happens next? You're right: six more issues suddenly appear. A first observation we have made in watching executives sort out such issues is that people in business are ambushed by different issues, something that continues relentlessly, day after day, and year after year.

However, if people were to "stop the world" at 10:01 a.m. and take stock or "take a picture" of the different issues on their desk, they would find only three types of issues that presented themselves over and over, each of which was associated with the element of time.

The first type of issue is one that comes from the past. When it lands on someone's desk or inbox, the event has already occurred. Why should an event that has already occurred end up on someone's list of things to do? Why should someone be concerned about an event that already happened? It is probably because the event represents something that has gone wrong, and this person is being asked to correct it. However, before being able to correct this situation, the individual needs to investigate what caused it to occur in the first place. This situation is called a *problem*, and the thought process required to solve it is called *Problem Analysis*. Problem Analysis is a diagnostic process developed by DPI to find the cause of an event that has gone wrong for unknown reasons. Therefore, as a person sorts through the issues on his or her desk, a pile of "problem" issues starts emerging.

A second stack consists of issues whereby a person is being told to "do something." However, there may be different things to do or different courses of action available. In other words, there are several alternatives or options available, and the best option is not evident because all the alternatives look reasonably good. In this instance, a person is working in the present tense and in a situation of choice. The thought process that will be used to bring the issue to a resolution is called *Decision Analysis*. Decision Analysis is a process used to choose the best option or course of action when several good ones are available.

The third pile that will form on a person's desk consists of issues in which a tentative decision has been made by someone in the organization, and this person's responsibility is to implement it successfully. With this goal in mind, a plan needs to be developed, and then looking ahead into the future, there is a need to anticipate any elements that may stand in the way of the plan's success. If these potential problems can be anticipated, one can develop actions to prevent them from occurring. This third thought process is called *Potential Problem Analysis*, and it is used to plan and implement decisions successfully.

Thus, an inventory of all the issues that face a person in business can be cataloged into three types—past, present, and future oriented—with each type requiring a different mode of thinking. The conscious application of the appropriate process to each issue is at the heart of rational decision making, and it is the key to getting issues resolved quickly and successfully.

DPI client Lee Tiong Peng, senior vice president at CapitaLand, describes it like this: "If you remove solving problems and making decisions from your daily work, what do you have left? Nothing! The primary driver of consistent performance is a proven, codified set of problem-solving and decision-making thinking processes that can be internalized as habit."

As technology and the pace of business continue to increase, the need for rapid and successful resolution is more important than ever:

• With modern technology, the ambush is now a 24/7 bombardment necessitating a need to empty the inventory quickly.
• There is a need for immediate response or action.
• The nature of the issues bombarding leaders has changed as business becomes more competitive and dynamic.

- Issues are now more often than not resolved by teams as opposed to individuals.

The boundary between operational and strategic issues has become more blurred for many. Here are some situations that leaders may have on their plate at any one moment of time:

- A competitor goes bankrupt.
- Another competitor enters the market.
- Management has announced a new pay-for-performance scheme.
- The department's star performer resigns.
- A major customer threatens to take her company's business elsewhere.
- A recommendation for a new Gizmo supplier needs to be prepared.
- The reason for falling Widget sales needs to be uncovered.
- A morale issue needs to be addressed.
- A replacement is needed for a key employee.

Situation Management provides a framework—a mental compass—for leaders and managers to situate themselves in the right process before they start any analysis. Just as a firefighter would use the appropriate technique to fight different types of fires, we apply different *mental toolkits* to process information about the past, present, and future. For example, thinking about the past requires us to process data about things that have already occurred, a very different skill than thinking about the future when we need think about issues that we wish to occur (or avoid).

First and foremost, since the role of all employees is to help the organization achieve its stated objectives, it is essential that the way managers deal with, and indeed prioritize, situations is aligned with the corporate direction. Beyond these benefits, and the millions of dollars that can be saved, many DPI clients have spoken of the soft benefits from the Situation Management Process. Said one client, "There's obviously an improvement in terms of saving dollars, reduced waste, and increased productivity, but there are some intangibles that we've found to be extremely beneficial. We now have a platform on which everyone is communicating on the same level."

Let's look at five of the component critical thinking processes of Situation Management that facilitate this.

SITUATION ANALYSIS

Situation Analysis is a process to help us do exactly what it says—take stock of the snapshot of situations requiring attention. If the remainder of the processes within Situation Management are essential, as they allow us (or our delegates) to "do things right," Situation Analysis is the most critical process, as its purpose is to make sure we "do the right things." Unfortunately, during the continuous bombardment of various situations, even savvy leaders can be sidetracked by burning issues of limited importance. Doing the right things right is not as trivial as it looks. Among the mistakes often made are these:

- Responding to existing situations to the exclusion of identifying *new* situations
- Diving into action before establishing clarity on the issues at hand
- Failing to prioritize effectively

Situation Analysis is a process that enables a leader to overcome these difficulties. Let's examine the steps of Situation Analysis.

STEP 1. SITUATIONS—IDENTIFYING ISSUES
Every person carries a list of issues or concerns that need to be dealt with. Some of us have a formal list—we keep it on our desk pad, diary, digital assistant, or smartphone, or we keep it as a list of things to do today. Many of us keep such a list informally,

in our heads. The first step of Situation Analysis involves this list of situations. We define a *situation* as a concern—whether threat or opportunity—that can have an impact on the results we are trying to achieve.

The situations step enables leaders to quickly identify and take stock of all the issues on their plate. The concerns could be delivered to us by somebody else—our boss, a subordinate, a customer—or proactively identified by us.

STEP 2. SEPARATION

Many of the issues that we need to address tend to be general; they are messy and fuzzy in nature. We therefore have to apply Caesar's principle of "Divide and conquer" in order to resolve each one. This is known as *separation*. It is the technique of breaking large, complex situations into smaller, more manageable ones. We separate fuzzy issues until we have discrete actionable issues that are distinct from each other and that can be handled on an individual basis.

STEP 3. PRIORITIZATION

Having accomplished the previous step of separation, we now have more issues to deal with. Since even Albert Einstein admitted that he could do only one thing at a time, and since that is true of us too, we must now set priorities on these issues. There are various ways of setting priorities. Let us look at some of the wrong ones.

There is the technique of *first-in, first-out,* which means that whatever came into the basket first gets immediate attention. There is the opposite concept of *last-in, first-out,* which means that the last item put into the basket gets immediate attention. A third is the technique of the *squeaky wheel.* Whoever yells the loudest gets his or her concern addressed first. A fourth technique is to *prioritize based on the requestor*—a situation from our boss is treated more importantly than one from a lower-ranking colleague. Likewise, the medium used may give undue priority to an issue. A message received by e-mail rather than by regular mail may receive higher priority. We may prioritize those things we like to do as opposed to those that we need to do.

If we want to set priorities correctly, there are three elements to examine. First, we should look at the *seriousness:*

- How important or serious is the issue?
- What are the, say, financial, safety, security, or reputation impacts of the issue?

Next, we should look at the *urgency*:

- What is the time deadline for resolving it?
- What urgency does it have?

Last, we should explore the *growth*:

- If we do nothing, what will happen to the seriousness?

While assessment of seriousness and urgency are relatively obvious factors to analyze for the rationally inclined, growth is often overlooked, but it is no less important, especially in the age of viral social media. The story of musician Dave Carroll and his spectacular YouTube hit "United Breaks Guitars" is a good example. Carroll's initial complaint to United Airlines about a guitar damaged on his flight may have appeared as low seriousness—it was an isolated case from one customer. Unfortunately for United, it had a high growth factor. When United failed to resolve the case to his satisfaction, Carroll uploaded his song and video on YouTube. The clip went viral, and within 24 hours it was picked up by CNN and other mainstream broadcasters, forcing United on to the back foot. As of December 2011, "United Breaks Guitars" had 11 million hits on YouTube and spawned two sequels. If United had been aware of the explosive growth factor that was waiting to be released, perhaps the airline would have treated Dave Carroll's complaint differently. How many Dave Carrolls are lurking in your CRM system?

Applying the three components of *seriousness*, *urgency*, and *growth* to each issue will help you set priorities correctly.

STEP 4. ALLOCATION

Once we have our concerns arranged in order of priority, the next step is to allocate each issue to the appropriate process of analysis and resolution. Three questions are used to do this:

> Question 1. Do we want to know the cause of this situation? If the answer is yes, then the process required for resolution is Problem Analysis.
> Question 2. Is there a need to select the best option? If we answer yes, then Decision Analysis is required.
> Question 3. Do we want to ensure the success of our plan? A yes would lead us to Potential Problem Analysis.

STEP 5. MANAGEMENT

Situation Analysis is the hub of our thinking. It is the mental compass of our logic map. It directs us to the proper analytical process in order to get issues and situations resolved successfully. However, to ensure that issues are followed through, there is the final step: *management.*

The management step is where we delegate the resolution of the issue to a colleague (if appropriate), clearly specify the result expected once the situation has been fully resolved, and establish a monitoring system to track progress.

PROBLEM ANALYSIS

Picture the stereotypical problem solvers. What do they look like? What types of problems do they solve? How do they go about it?

Many of our clients picture the production supervisors, complete with nametags and clipboards! Or they're mechanics complete with toolboxes who'll come and fix the machines when they're broken. In all of these cases the "problems" are with tangible things—machines, for example—and the problem solvers use their intimate knowledge of the machines to fix them. You might say that the problem solvers rely more on experience and expertise than on any "thinking process."

The reality of today of course is quite different. Problems may feature "things," but they are just as likely to be about "soft items" including people, sales figures, efficiency, or productivity. Gathering and filtering relevant information about such issues is a primary challenge of effective problem solving. We need a process to help us do this and drive our analysis to the most suitable course of action.

In the language of Situation Management, a *problem* is a deviation of performance away from the norm for which the cause is unknown and is thus of concern.

In resolving problems, we situate ourselves in the past. When we talk about analyzing a problem situation, we want to go from problem to action. Whenever a problem occurs, we need to answer the question, "What are we going to do about it?"

The pressure to be seen as doing something will lead gung-ho leaders to dive in and, on occasion, "do anything." This often only makes matters worse. What is required is an efficient way to rapidly "join the dots" between the symptoms of the problem we observe—for example, a sudden fall in the sales of product ABC or high rejects in process XYZ—and the cause of these symptoms. Once the cause has been identified, suitable actions can be put in place.

Given that most significant problems are resolved by teams, there are a number of difficulties to overcome when resolving problems:

1. An inability to agree on exactly what the problem is
2. Difficulty in rapidly organizing the data associated with the problem into a format that can be properly analyzed

3. Key data about the problem being missing

4. Inability to isolate relevant changes that may have contributed to the problem, leading to a "brute-force" approach to problem solving

5. Taking actions to "undo" changes instead of inspecting how those changes may have caused the problem (which could lead to a far superior resolution)

To avoid these pitfalls, there are a number of steps that we may have to pursue along the way. This is called the logic path of *Problem Analysis.*

Those thinking that the approach that follows is overkill may do well to learn from the millions of dollars DPI's clients have saved from this process. We can attribute tens of thousands in savings to their ability to scrutinize the seat-of-the-pants recommendations of mechanics and air-conditioning engineers. One U.S.-based client saved $2.3 million through the use of Problem Analysis on only one of their six production lines. A team of non-IT professionals working with an insurance client in Malaysia generated a solution to an IT problem (that the IT folks couldn't) with a payback period of only three months!

Let us now take a look at the skills involved in each step of Problem Analysis.

STEP 1. IDENTIFICATION

The first step is, of course, identification: "How do I know I have a problem?" One way of looking at a problem is to say that some obstacle is interfering with the attainment of some goal or that some deviation has occurred in the expected performance, or norm. The first element involved is to identify the norm. Another element that is involved is the knowledge of what is actually being achieved or what is actually happening.

When the norm and the actual are one and the same, there is no problem. When the actual is lower than the norm, however, we have a *negative deviation.* When the actual is above the norm, then we have a *positive deviation*. This leads to a subtle but important point. Unlike in everyday language, within the framework of Situation Management, a problem is not necessarily negative. Positive deviations, such as a much lower than expected rate of attrition in the East Coast sales team, can be analyzed with Problem Analysis, with the obvious intent to identify the cause behind the success and then replicate it elsewhere.

The first thing we will notice about the deviation is its effects. However, in order to correct a deviation, we need to find the cause. To do that, we must proceed to a description of the problem.

STEP 2. DESCRIPTION

Of the conscious or subconscious steps of Problem Analysis, this step is the one most frequently overlooked, done in a cursory manner, or done out of sequence. We suspect this is driven by two factors:

1. The inherent desire to take "action" (the last step!)
2. A false belief that if we have clearly identified the problem, then we have adequately "got our hands around it"

The description step is critical because of the following:

- It will eliminate superfluous or irrelevant (perhaps hysterical) information that might otherwise derail our activities.
- It allows us to clearly spot the "information gaps" we need to fill, and to discover what we don't know.
- It enables us to conduct thorough analysis of the problem.
- It forms the basis on which possible causes will be established.
- It allows us to test possible causes (deductive logic, not physical testing) so we can quickly isolate the most probable cause.

If you're observant as you read the remainder of this section, you'll realize that embedded in the above list are three subsequent steps of Problem Analysis that rely solely on the quality of the description. Therefore, fully describing the problem is of critical importance. This is not as easy as it sounds since, unlike Christmas presents, business problems do not come nicely gift-wrapped. The factual data about them is usually fractured, poorly organized, or missing. The purpose of the description step is to collect and organize the *relevant* facts about the problem.

To properly describe a problem, there are four dimensions about which we can get some information. These are the *identity, location, timing,* and *extent of the problem.*

By carefully examining these four dimensions, we can ensure that we properly describe the problem. And, if there are any gaps, at least we know where to look to fill them.

In among the questions above are questions that seek to describe the problem in terms of what it is (*problem area*) and what it is not (*non-problem area*). The initial reaction of many is that this is a weird and confusing thing to do. In fact, it is highly intuitive analysis that most people do naturally but without knowing it. Here are some not-so-obvious but common ways in which we subconsciously practice *is* versus *is not* thinking:

- You are watching TV, and the screen suddenly goes blank. Your natural behavior is to first (and almost instantly) verify that the lights or other electronic devices are on (that is, verify that the problem *is not* an electricity failure). Second, you would switch channels to see if they are working. By doing this, you could conclude that the problem *is* channel A, but it *is not* any other channel.
- You notice that there is a series of scratches on the rear passenger-side door of your car. You would then inspect the front doors and the rear driver-side door for scratches. As a result, you could conclude that the *what* of the problem *is* the rear off-side door, and it *is not* any other door.

- When you go to a doctor with stomach pain, she will no doubt prod you and use your screams of agony to determine where the limits of the pain are (that is, where the pain *is* and where it *is not*).

By describing the problem in terms of *what, where, when,* and *how much* it *is* and *is not,* we are able to put sharper boundaries around the problem. These boundaries will help us through the next steps:

- They will help us isolate differences.
- They will provide a test bed for eliminating possible causes during the testing step.

STEP 3. ANALYSIS

"Something must be *different* about this particular item," says one team member. "Yes, or something has *changed* along the way," replies another. The concepts of *differences* and *changes* are intuitively understood to be a part of the problem-solving process. The purpose of the analysis step is to rapidly isolate relevant differences and changes.

The first part of the analysis step is to compare the problem area to the non-problem area, or, in other words, the *is* to the *is not.* We can *compare for similarities,* or we can *compare for differences.* In looking for new and additional information, experience has shown that comparing for differences is more helpful. In particular, we should examine our description to look for differences in areas in which there are sharp contrasts in the information.

The next step is to examine the differences in order to identify changes that have occurred. The search for the cause must center itself on these changes. If no change had occurred, we would not have a problem. To narrow our search for relevant changes, we should limit our search to looking for changes within the differences that we have identified between the problem area and the non-problem area. The reason is that any change to a nondifference would impact the problem and non-problem areas equally; hence it could not be related to the problem. We need to answer the question, "What has changed about each of these differences?" Noting the date or time of each change is also helpful because we might be able to relate the start of a problem to a specific change that occurred.

STEP 4. HYPOTHESES

This is when we really need to put our thinking caps on. Thus far, we've been dealing with factual information. Now, we need to review the differences and changes to develop *hypotheses* (also known as *possible causes*) for the problem.

From our analysis of the deviation, we can now formulate some hypotheses as to the possible causes of the deviation. A *hypothesis* is a synthesis of the changes and differences identified with the experience and expertise of the problem-solving team.

It is important to emphasize that a hypothesis is not the same as a change. It is not adequate to say, "A possible cause of this problem is that the manager involved changed." The purpose is to draw a link between the differences and/or changes and the problem effects we have observed. A hypothesis must explain *how* differences and/or changes could lead to the problem. At this stage, we list all reasonable hypotheses. The emphasis is to be constructive and to make the best use of our experience and expertise.

STEP 5. TESTS

This is when the effort we put into the description step pays huge dividends. We are able to mentally test, by the process of deductive logic, each of the possible causes we've identified. We do this by measuring each possible cause against the problem description.

In order to eliminate those that are not related to the problem, we screen each possible cause through our description. If a possible cause cannot explain both sides of the description, it is not likely to be the real cause. Some possible causes might do so if we add certain assumptions (*only if*). In such cases these assumptions should be noted.

The testing technique is as follows:

- Test each possible cause through the test bed (description), especially the sharp contrast areas.
- Note all assumptions (*only if*) that you have to construct to support your hypotheses.

The most probable cause will be the one that best explains the description, or the one with the least number of assumptions. To be 100 percent certain, we must now verify our assumptions—which should be done quickly and cheaply.

Should these assumptions prove to be true, we have the root cause of the problem and are ready to take action.

STEP 6. ACTION

To address a problem, we can take three different types of action:

Interim action. This is used to buy us time while we search out the cause of the problem. Interim action is aimed at the effects of the problem.

Adaptive action. We decide to live with the problem or adapt ourselves to the problem. Adaptive action is also aimed at the effects of the problem.

Corrective action. This is the only action designed to eliminate the problem. It is aimed at eliminating the cause of the problem.

From a conceptual perspective corrective action is the superior course of action to take, and it is fair to say that we should try to seek out and implement a corrective action wherever possible. However, there are valid reasons why this may not be possible.

Under intense circumstances, we may be forced to take interim action while a full and proper investigation takes place. An example would be a bank whose ATM network failed. In such circumstances, when millions of customers are inconvenienced, it is necessary to take interim action to get the system up and running again first. The pitfall to avoid is forgetting to complete a proper investigation and let a "Band-Aid solution" become permanent!

An adaptive action could be appropriate if the price of a corrective action exceeds the costs of the problem. In this case, there would be no business case for a corrective action. A simple example could be a bad carpet stain that cannot be removed: rather than replacing the entire carpet, we may rightly choose to cover the offending stain with a suitable rug or chair.

DECISION ANALYSIS

Let us now, for a moment, situate ourselves mentally in the present.

After we have explored the past to identify the cause of the problem, it is necessary to choose the appropriate course of action to address that problem. This next step in decision making is known as *Decision Analysis*. The overall objective in this process is to take several alternatives and choose the best one.

Decision Analysis can help guard against difficulties such as these:

- Being faced with too many choices, many of which might be of different categories
- Failing to analyze the downsides associated with the alternatives
- Gravitating toward historical precedents or "pet favorite" alternatives

Decision Analysis comprises five steps.

STEP 1. DECISION OBJECTIVE

There are three elements of the decision objective or decision statement that we should keep in mind. The first element is the purpose. A decision statement should be formulated in terms that represent the purpose of what the analysis is about. It should represent an end result. As an example to demonstrate the process, let us assume that you have been mandated with the following decision by your company: Choose the best laptop computer.

From time to time we may insert in our decision statement a word that restricts the range of alternatives that will be available to us. These words are called *modifiers*. Without modifiers, the range of alternatives would be broader. However, by adding a modifier, we restrict the range. It is important to make sure when we formulate decision statements to examine them for modifiers to ensure that we do in fact want to include them. In the above example, we might wish to include the term "WinTel," which obviously would eliminate Apple or Linux laptop computers.

The third element to consider about the decision objective or decision statement is the level of the decision. Most decisions stem from prior decisions: the choice cascade. The higher the level of our decision, the greater the range of alternatives available to us. The lower the level, the more restricted is the range of alternatives. The level at which we start our decision dramatically changes the class of alternatives that we end up comparing. It enables us to compare similar classes of alternatives so that we compare apples to apples and not apples to oranges.

Considering the level of our decision, or more specifically, the prior decisions that have already been taken, enables us to overcome two major pitfalls in decision making. First, it helps us uncover and question any implicit decisions we have made or any assumptions we have made. Returning to the laptop example, a prior decision that is implied by "Choose the best laptop computer" is that it has already been decided that a laptop computer is required. If this is an invalid assumption, the decision objective could be changed to "Choose the best computer."

Second, in circumstances where management has delegated a recommendation to us, we can uncover the prior decisions taken by management and then factor these into our recommendation so that we are in step with management. There are many possible prior decisions in the example of "Choose the best laptop computer." Management may have decided that the current brand is too expensive or that the current model is not "cool" enough for the new company brand or that it can be offered as a prize at the "Dinner and Dance." Each of these prior decisions would lead to a different set of selection criteria at the next step. To ensure that we are aligned with management (not the same thing as reverse engineering our rationale to be "subservient" to them), it is critical to make their prior decisions explicit and to challenge them if warranted (to make the choice cascade visible).

A lack of appreciation of the decision-level concept can explain why:

- Senior management complain that their staff are not aligned with the strategy or "big picture"
- Apparently solid recommendations get rejected by management
- Those "sure-win" sales are lost

STEP 2. SELECTION CRITERIA

The second step in Decision Analysis is to establish some criteria for selecting the best alternative. To generate effective selection criteria, we must be aware of the underlying rationale for the decision being made, and then we must ask four questions:

Question 1. What results do we want to achieve?

Question 2. What results do we want to avoid?

Question 3. What resources are available to spend?

Question 4. What resources do we want to preserve?

These questions ensure that we've covered all the bases. For example, it is human nature to think about what we want and to overlook those things that we do not want.

Once we have a list of selection criteria, we examine them to determine the criteria that are absolutely mandatory to the success of our decision. We classify our criteria into those that must absolutely be met and those that we want to achieve—that are desirable but not mandatory. The first criteria we list are the *musts*—those that are imperative and must be met by all available alternatives.

Then we take a look at the desirable criteria, or the *wants*, and weigh them in order of importance. By looking at our desirable criteria, we identify the one that is the most important to us and give it a weight of 10. With that as the benchmark, we weigh the others on a scale of 10 to 1, according to their relative importance.

STEP 3. COMPARING THE ALTERNATIVES

The next step in the process of Decision Analysis is the step of comparing the alternatives. We must filter the alternatives through the selection criteria and eliminate those that do not measure up. Because we have classified our criteria into musts and wants, the first filter is to screen the alternatives against the musts.

Since we have set specific limits on these musts, we need to gather information about each alternative to see how well it complies with them. By comparing the information that is available about each alternative against each must, we can then make a *go/no go decision*. *Go* means that the alternative meets the limits that we have determined to be nonnegotiable, and *no go* means that the alternative does not. The purpose of must criteria is to quickly screen out those alternatives that violate the limits that we consider nonnegotiable, thereby reducing our range of alternatives.

The next step is to compare the remaining alternatives against the wants, or the desirable criteria. Again, the technique is to get information about the alternative that tells us how well it performs against each of our wants. We then use our judgment in assessing that information in order to score the performance of each alternative against each want. Using numbers to reflect our judgment, we give the top score to the alternative that performs the best followed by relative scores to each of the subsequent next best performing alternatives. We then proceed to do that against each want. By then multiplying the weight of the wants by the score of the alternative, we get a weighted score. We repeat the procedure for each want. Adding the total of these weighted scores gives us an *index of performance*.

In the compare alternatives step, our musts criteria eliminate unsuitable options, and our wants criteria compare what is left, letting the cream rise to the top. By now, we will have narrowed our choice down to one, two, or possibly three alternatives that perform substantially better than the rest.

STEP 4. RISK EVALUATION

The next step in Decision Analysis is the step called *risk evaluation*. Every alternative or course of action considered brings with it certain risks. Therefore, in the analysis of the alternatives, it is very important to evaluate the risks that are attached to each of these remaining alternatives. The technique is simple. We take each alternative and ask, "What risks do we face if we go with this alternative?" We list those risks. We do this for each of the remaining alternatives.

The risks will be different for each alternative because different alternatives bring different risks. However, there are different degrees of risk. First we look at the degree of probability that any of these risks will come about. Using a scale of high, medium, or low, or of 1 to 10, we examine each risk and assess its probability of occurrence. The next element in determining the degree of risk is to determine the degree of seriousness should it occur. If this risk occurs, what will be the impact of our particular decision? Using the same scale, we can then assess the degree of seriousness for each risk.

STEP 5. THE BEST-BALANCED CHOICE

The last step of Decision Analysis is making the *best-balanced choice*. This means reviewing the risks that are represented by the probability and the seriousness. If our comfort level is such that we are not willing to undertake high risk, we would then have to choose an alternative that has attached to it a degree of risk with which we are comfortable. The best-balanced choice becomes the alternative that performs the best, or reasonably well, against our selection criteria, together with the amount of risk that we are willing to accept.

POTENTIAL PROBLEM ANALYSIS

Let us now situate ourselves mentally in the future. Obviously, we want the future to be successful for us; this is why we need *Potential Problem Analysis* (PPA). Potential Problem Analysis comes into play to implement the decision we have made in the previous step, or to implement a decision that was taken by management and then passed to us for execution.

The central tenet of Potential Problem Analysis is captured in the famous saying "An ounce of prevention is worth a pound of cure." Sadly, due to Figure 10.1's all-too-familiar vicious cycle of poor thinking, we don't have time to prevent! Potential Problem Analysis is a great way to break through this unproductive pattern.

STEP 1. SUCCESS STATEMENT

The principle of Potential Problem Analysis is to help us successfully implement a chosen course of action. We begin with a *success statement*.

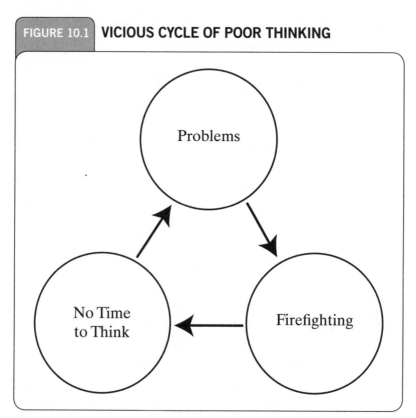

FIGURE 10.1 VICIOUS CYCLE OF POOR THINKING

While the need for a success statement is obvious enough—we want to know in advance what success "looks like"—establishing an effective success statement requires it to be SMART: *specific, measurable, agreed and documented, realistic, and time-bound.*

Moreover, in today's age being smart is not good enough! We need to be SMARTER, where the E stands for *end outcome* (as opposed to an intermediate step), and the R is for *relevant* (if not, why bother doing it?).

STEP 2. THE PLAN

Our next step is to develop a plan and list its steps in chronological order, including who is accountable for each step and when it should be completed by. Note that the accountable individual must not be a group or department, but what we call a *single warm body*—for example, James Lee or Michael Siew. This individual isn't necessarily working alone and may have a team of others who will contribute. Nevertheless, the accountable party is the individual who must ensure that the task is completed, and it is the individual whom the overall leader would approach to monitor progress.

STEP 3. HIGH-RISK AREAS

At this stage it is important to identify the steps that are of critical importance to the plan's success.

We identify the *high-risk areas* by examining the critical areas of the plan for potential problems. Here are some of the not-so-obvious areas of high risk:

- Steps that have never been done before
- Steps with overlapping authority
- Steps that require teams or individuals who have not worked together before to successfully collaborate
- Steps on a particularly aggressive timeline

The amount of risk is then identified by looking at the probability and seriousness of each potential problem.

STEP 4. PREVENTION

Prevention is next. We can take *preventive actions* that are directed at the high-probability causes. We try to anticipate the likely causes of each potential problem together with the probability that each will occur. Preventive actions reduce the probability that a problem will occur, and they are taken in advance of the problem's happening. In other words, our aim is to identify specific actions we can take to prevent a likely cause from actually happening, thereby preventing the potential problem itself. We do not target our preventive actions at the problem itself.

If a potential problem has many likely causes, we must develop a preventive action (or actions) for each of the causes we believe might actually come to pass.

STEP 5. PROTECTION

If our preventive actions fail and the potential problems materialize, we will need actions to protect us against the seriousness of the effects of the problem. These are called *contingent actions* because they come into play after the problem has occurred.

Sometimes, our best efforts at preventing a potential problem do not work, or perhaps, in rare circumstances it is simply not possible to develop a preventive action at all.

We need to develop contingent actions to minimize the impact of the potential problem. In other words, unlike preventive actions that reduce the probability of a potential problem's occurring, contingent actions minimize the seriousness of a problem if it does occur.

Although the ability to "think on our feet" might be considered an asset, this is not an excuse not to develop our contingent actions in advance. What we do need though is a trigger that will indicate when we need to execute a particular contingent action.

STEP 6. THE MODIFIED PLAN

The last step of Potential Problem Analysis is to take our original plan and to modify it by inserting, at the appropriate steps, the best selection of preventive and contingent actions. These should reduce the potential risk to a level that is acceptable. The *modified plan* is the one to implement because it has a higher probability of succeeding than the original one.

THE CREATIVE PROCESS

The leader who works to address operational situations will confront circumstances in which, for example:

- An existing set of alternative actions are inadequate.
- A team is struggling to turn threats into opportunities.
- None of the possible causes in a problem situation adequately describe the problem.
- Some "out-of-the-box" preventive actions are needed for apparently uncontrollable risks.

In such circumstances the leader needs to develop some newer, fresher ideas. Unfortunately, there are many barriers to creativity. The purpose of the creative process is to overcome these barriers.

Many tomes have been written on this subject of barriers to creativity. To summarize some of the main research findings, it has been shown that we have two parts of the brain: the left brain and the right brain. The left side is analytical, logical, and rational, whereas the right brain is intuitive, artistic, and creative. The majority of *adults* (not necessarily so true of children!) are left brain dominant. That is, our logical thought processes dominate the creative ones, often subconsciously. You might have experienced your left brain talking to you: "This idea would never work," or "John's so crazy," or "The numbers don't stack up."

There are a number of reasons adults tend to be left brain dominant. For want of a better word, we adults have a lot of "baggage." Our experience has shown us that things don't always work, which can generate a "fear of failure" or a "set of rules" that we follow. In addition, education, and indeed society as a whole, reinforces left brain thinking. Laws, morals, and social graces are all left brain oriented.

To overcome these barriers and to translate the ideas subsequently generated into action, the five steps of the creative process are required.

STEP 1. PREPARATION

Have you ever been called into a "brainstorming" session at short notice and the whole thing rapidly went flat? That doesn't do much to boost your confidence in creativity, does it?

The preparation step requires the leader to do the following:

- Be clear what we want to be creative about
- Set the right physical environment
- Establish an appropriate emotional environment
- Get the right people involved
- Prime the right brain of those people with appropriate warm-up exercises

STEP 2. GENERATION

Generation involves divergent thinking and thus follows a "quantity, not quality" mantra—just as digging for and finding diamonds requires that a lot of earth be dug up.

The most well known generation technique is brainstorming, first developed by advertising executive Alex Osborn in 1942. Done well, brainstorming can be effective, but most leaders are unaware of how to conduct an effective brainstorming session. We advise leaders to be clear on the respective roles in the session, set a time limit of around 20 minutes for idea generation, and set a stretch target of ideas to be generated in that time.

Often, even with the best of preparation, brainstorming may not yield the desired results. "Old hat" ideas may result. *Creative stimulators* can be used to overcome this.

The basic premise behind stimulators is to change the context of the situation, which helps to remove barriers, thus enabling more ideas to emerge. In doing so, stimulators tend to generate a smaller number of ideas, but they are more specific ideas and "fresh."

There are seven stimulators often used by DPI consultants:

1. *Random words.* To draw upon associations of words unrelated to the creative topic
2. *Transformation.* To ask the question "What if?" in relation to your topic

3. *Reversal.* To look at the creative topic from a 180 degree angle
4. *Boundary distortion.* To deliberately "put your backs against the wall" and see what the "desperation" throws up
5. *Intermediate impossible.* To consciously remove potential barriers
6. *Force field.* To tear apart the creative topic and identify high-impact areas
7. *Wishing.* To dream up an ideal scenario and then figure out what it would take to make this scenario a reality

Appropriate use of stimulators will make the difference between success and failure of the generation step.

STEP 3. SYNTHESIS

The *synthesis step* is when the left brain kicks back in order to transform the rough ideas generated into workable concepts that can actually be implemented.

The first thing to do is to scan through the list of ideas and remove any duplicates. Next, we refine, where possible, unethical, socially unacceptable, or impractical ideas into something viable. For example, while it may be impractical to have the Queen of England attend a product launch, engaging a look-alike is a possibility. Ideas that cannot be suitably refined are discarded. Finally, we group ideas together into common categories, or wherever possible, link ideas together, to develop a few *super alternative concepts*, which are richer than any of the component ideas generated at the prior step.

STEP 4. VERIFICATION

After the synthesis step, we are left with a manageable number of workable concepts. Now we are faced with the choice of selecting which ones to implement. The skills of Decision Analysis are applied here.

STEP 5. IMPLEMENTATION

Once we've decided which ideas to implement, we must do so successfully. At this point, Potential Problem Analysis is invaluable.

SUMMARY

The component processes of Situation Management allow leaders and their teams to manage day-to-day issues in a time-effective and strategically aligned manner.

Depending on the circumstances, the processes may be deployed in full, including a complete set of process instruments, tools, checklists, worksheets, and so on, or they may be implemented into the organization informally, through the questions that all staff members are expected to ask and answer as a part of their daily work.

We address the topic of implementation in more detail in the next chapter.

CHAPTER 11

Increasing the Situation Management Quotient of the Organization

A s will be shown in more detail in the following chapters, the best way to implement processes such as Situation Management is through the comprehensive introduction of the core processes into homogeneous groups. That is, the desired outcome is one of culture change as opposed to "learning," which is the objective of ad hoc training or briefing sessions.

SUCCESSFULLY IMPLEMENTING SITUATION MANAGEMENT PROCESSES

With this in mind, there are four critical steps in the successful implementation of the Situation Management Processes in an organization:

> Step 1. Management participates in, is committed to, and owns the processes.
>
> Step 2. A critical mass of people learn and apply the processes in homogeneous work groups.
>
> Step 3. There is ongoing application of the processes to real-life situations.
>
> Step 4. People are assisted in turning the processes into habits, preferably through trained internal consultants.

Step 1 is obvious enough: not only must management take responsibility for the change but they must also practice what they preach. If they don't participate in the active deployment and use of the processes themselves, people at lower levels will rightly conclude that there is no value in using the processes themselves.

Step 2 is also based on sound common sense. If you lack critical mass, the language underlying the new processes will be lost simply because not enough people can speak it. If the language is restricted to a special few, they will find it impossible to converse with their colleagues, and they will revert to the old forms of working and communication.

Furthermore, the concepts should be learned against the backdrop of the real issues the homogenous teams face. It may be educational to work on the historical problems of others, but any skill building exercise based on such a foundation will lack traction, as the most natural reaction is "But my issues are different." Only by applying new concepts to real issues, and immediately realizing the benefits of the concepts in practical application, will this skill building generate the momentum sufficient for ongoing application.

Step 3 is simply to build on the successes achieved at step 2. The simple but effective mantra is "Success builds success."

Step 4 recognizes the obvious fact that new skills are not mastered overnight. Just as an exercise routine is more successful when accompanied by a coach who can cajole and encourage the exerciser and immediately rectify his or her errors, the learning of new thinking processes requires a *process facilitator* who immediately addresses any difficulties that would have participants reverting to the old ways and who corrects any bad habits before they become ingrained.

Table 11.1 contains an outline of a general implementation plan. Implementation involves key parties who perform a variety of important roles, as listed in Table 11.2.

TABLE 11.1

NUMBER	ELEMENT	KEY ACTIVITIES
Step 1	Implementation structuring	• Overview orientation meeting • Population identification • Objectives and key issues agreed upon • Selection of implementation coordinator
Step 2	Management familiarization workshop	• Executive management workshop (two to three days)
Step 3	Internal trainers' development	• Selection of instructor candidates • Instructor training program • First program observation and support • Ongoing coaching and support

(continued on next page)

TABLE 11.1	*(continued)*	
NUMBER	**ELEMENT**	**KEY ACTIVITIES**
Step 4	Ongoing schedule of workshops	• Scheduling of workshops and participants • Coordination of facilities, materials, and trainers • Identification of issues and participants • Evaluation
Step 5	Development of internal consultants	• Selection of proposed process facilitators and/or consultants • Consulting skills development • Ongoing coaching and support

TABLE 11.2	
Senior managers	Visibly sponsor and use the processes; encourage application; make people available for workshops; ensure adequate budget
Program coordinators	Coordinate execution of workshop schedule; monitor instructors' effectiveness; ensure adequate follow-up and maintenance
Program instructors	Workshop leaders; coach the participants concerning process application; modify presentations to suit audience
Process consultants	Process leaders on specific issues; process advisors to working groups; process coaches to managers and others
External consultants such as those from DPI	Develop internal resources; supply materials and methodology; provide ongoing support and evaluation, as well as counsel; act as external process consultants

Of course, there are many nuances that must be successfully navigated to ensure success. One such nuance is process emphasis, which is important since no one is suggesting that the CEO be equipped with exactly the same skills as the production line manager. Rather, the common framework, language, and processes are differentiated according to level, by varying emphasis, context, and application (see Figure 11.1).

Emphasis also serves another important function, which is to ensure that the time and financial investment are commensurate with the level of management.

In summary, implementation consists of a program in which an independent consultant, for example, DPI, provides the methodology, acts as the initial catalyst, and ultimately helps guide the client to take ownership of the processes.

SITUATION MANAGEMENT AS A STRATEGY CASCADE

In all of the strategy assignments we undertake, a similar Critical Issue pops up. It is variously described as one of the following:

- Transformational leadership
- Cultural change
- Strategic alignment

Whatever the specifics of the language used, the common intent is to cascade the strategy down the levels of an organization in order to encourage new desired behaviors at all levels. A common but ultimately doomed approach to try to achieve this is the infamous "town hall meeting," complete with snazzy presentations, special effects worthy of David Copperfield, and an overly enthusiastic leadership team. Despite all the gloss, these events rely on the same underlying engagement and learning method that is universally agreed as the least effective: telling.

FIGURE 11.1 **PROCESS EMPHASIS: EMPHASIS CHANGES WITH LEVEL OF MANAGEMENT**

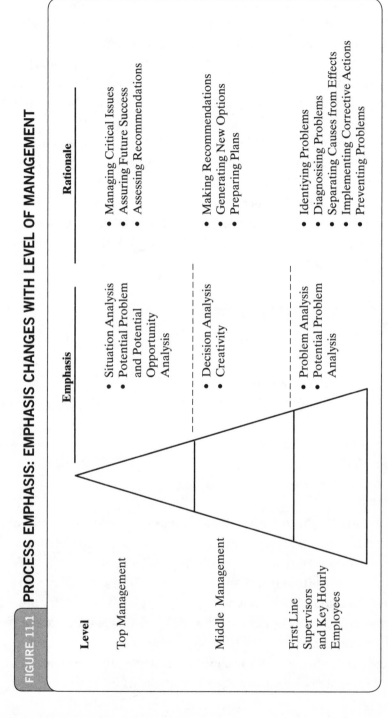

Level	Emphasis	Rationale
Top Management	• Situation Analysis • Potential Problem and Potential Opportunity Analysis	• Managing Critical Issues • Assuring Future Success • Assessing Recommendations
Middle Management	• Decision Analysis • Creativity	• Making Recommendations • Generating New Options • Preparing Plans
First Line Supervisors and Key Hourly Employees	• Problem Analysis • Potential Problem Analysis	• Identifying Problems • Diagnosing Problems • Separating Causes from Effects • Implementing Corrective Actions • Preventing Problems

Most intended recipients, for various reasons ranging from boredom to illness to failing to watch the webcast, won't "get it." Those that do will be left with the same burning question: "I'm now aware of the *what*, but am I equipped with the *how*?"

The town hall meeting approach is akin to a coach's saying to his athletes "You need to run faster" without conveying the running skills required to run faster (for example, raising the knees or using different breathing patterns). Of course, most coaches would not do that to their players, but management does it to the troops time and again.

Since the Situation Management Processes are basically how-to tools, many of our clients adopt a far more effective approach. They structure a strategic change initiative around the Situation Management framework. One client designed a strategic engagement program entitled Achieving Change Through Situation Management. This program encompasses the rollout of a four-phase workshop approach as follows:

Phase 1. A half-day engagement session with homogeneous groups in which the premise of the strategy—for example, to review hiring practices—is discussed and then translated into operable terms relevant to the level of the groups. The participants need to answer the question, "What do we now need to do differently?" from which a suitable change project is identified.

Phase 2. A two- or three-day workshop in which the Situation Management Processes are learned and applied to the change projects, resulting in first-cut recommendations.

Phase 3. A period of coaching as the teams refine the recommendations associated with their change project.

Phase 4. Presentations to management in which "go" decisions are sought based on the Decision Analysis logic path of the recommendations that are clearly and succinctly laid out to management.

There are two outcomes of this approach:

1. The strategy is cascaded into operable terms throughout the organization.
2. The staff is equipped with decision-making skills to live up to the strategy.

SUMMARY

Treating the deployment of a critical thinking process such as Situation Management into an organization as a "training exercise" is missing a trick. As will be described in the next chapter, training is often perceived as a necessary evil or viewed with suspicion by management and staff alike. The days when training classes would regularly run for three or four days to thoroughly examine a topic and rigorously apply the new skills in real time are dwindling. Instead, the typical training mindset that prevails today is, "What is the shortest amount of time in which it can be done?" and "What is the lowest cost?" Hidden in this view is the underlying belief that the training time, in and of itself, is of little value.

At DPI we've been practicing our belief in hands-on, practical, and work-oriented workshops for the last 35 years. Delivered properly, as described above, staff members in such programs are not being "dragged away from productive work" but are actually being more productive by working on real issues in a focused and facilitated manner.

PART 5

THE LEADER AS PROCESS COACH AND MANAGER

CHAPTER 12

Self-Mastery

Beffore any process can be implemented, it must first be mastered by those suggesting its implementation.

When a group of executives is asked to name leaders they admire, depending on where they are in the world the list is likely to include some or all of the following familiar names:

- Steve Jobs (Americas)
- Ho Ching (Asia)
- Michael O'Leary (Europe)
- Tony Fernandez (Asia)
- Graham McKay (Africa)
- Richard Branson (Europe)
- Warren Buffett (Americas)
- Nelson Mandela (Africa)
- GT Ferreira, Laurie Dippenaar, and Paul Harris (Africa)
- Oprah Winfrey (Americas)

For better or worse, we live in the era of the celebrity CEO, so much so that many have speculated as to Apple's fate in the post-Jobs era. After all, "He was the company" some would say. Time will tell how Apple fares, but we suspect its new chief executive Tim Cook will do just fine.

While many may conclude that these celebrities possess superhuman-like powers that make them such renowned leaders, at DPI we believe that these individuals have simply mastered the processes we describe in this book and have successfully infused them throughout their entire organizations.

Self-mastery of any skill is a prerequisite to any attempt to transfer the skill to others. Self-mastery requires the conscious and visible application of a skill. In the realm of critical thinking, that may seem a little strange. It is in the very nature of the human psyche to be a thinker. "That is what makes us human" may be a typical response. Of course, that is true. The careful observation of children at any age will reveal their inner thinker. So the question is not whether we can think but whether we can think *critically and consciously.*

If all this sounds a little deep, let's explore a suitable analogy. Every human being on this planet can breathe. Any parent knows that it is the first breath that indicates the successful emergence of a new life. In other words, we are all born with a default level of breathing capability, at the subconscious level, which is perfectly adequate for most people.

However, there are professions in which this default level of breathing is insufficient. Examples include singing, sports, music (wind instruments), martial arts, professional speaking, and yoga. Those that make their living in these professions take tangible steps to study the art of breathing, and its underlying mechanics, to enable them to excel. Michael Phelps famously won eight gold medals at the 2008 Olympics, but it is little remembered that the seventh gold was obtained at a margin of only 0.01 seconds. For him the difference between being "the Olympian" with a permanent place in the history books and being "a failure" (to beat Spitz) came down to the length of a fingernail. There is no doubt in our minds that his ability to fine-tune his breathing was an important contributor to his success. For individuals like Phelps, "default" breathing is a nonstarter. The lesson: Anyone has the option to take control of his or her breathing, to learn specific breathing skills, but few bother.

Our contention is that critical thinking is the "breathing" of leadership. Yes, everyone can think, but the default level of thinking we are born with is not sufficient. To be a true leader, like those listed earlier, the executive must take steps to learn the art and science of thinking, and he or she must consciously master and apply specific thinking techniques (we call them *processes*) in response to the matters at hand.

Self-mastery will appear as an ability when the following occur:

When Promoting a View, Leaders Will Be Able To
- Explain their rationale and its underlying data.
- Encourage others to challenge and/or validate their view.
- Encourage others to provide different views (for example, "Do you have either different data, different conclusions, or both?").

When Inquiring into Another's Views, Leaders Will Be Able To
- Actively seek to understand the other's views by asking the right questions.
- Explore ways the views differ to others.
- Uncover the train of thought, or "logic flow," that led up to the views.

Having Expanded Their Sphere of Influence, Leaders Will Be Able To
- Coach those around them, to equip them with the same level of conscious thought that they possess.
- Establish the systems and procedures that will encourage critical thought throughout the entire organization.

We deal with these topics in turn in the next two chapters.

CHAPTER 13

The Leader as Critical Thinking Coach

Business is decision making! Every day, hundreds if not thousands of decisions are being made that will directly impact both the financial performance of the organization and its ability to achieve the future "look and direction" desired by the CEO. Simply put, the success and failure of any organization rests on the quality of the thousands of decisions made and implemented every day, every week, and every month.

As has been observed already, the winning organization of the future will be the one that can out-think the competition. This out-thinking shouldn't be restricted to the top echelons of management, so the leader must take steps to be a coach. As the famous saying goes, "Give a man a fish and you feed him for a day. Teach a man how to fish and you feed him for a lifetime."

Many decisions will require the sign-off or approval of the leader. In this capacity the leader is either evaluating these recommendations or influencing how such decisions are arrived at. In this capacity, the leader must be the *critical thinking coach* of the organization.

However, the overwhelming majority of decisions made in any organization require limited or no involvement of the leader. The clear implication is that the leader's influence on the decision-making culture of the organization must be felt beyond his or her direct involvement. The leader must take steps to set the tone and establish the desired decision-making culture of the organization. This is covered in the next chapter.

CRITICAL THINKING COACH

The first prerequisite for critical thinking coaches is for them to be process and systems thinkers. They must be consciously aware of the thinking processes they and others follow. Many leaders are unable to fulfill this, as their thinking is at a subconscious level, and they attribute their decision-making ability to "gut feel" or "intuition." Unfortunately, it is impossible for them to pass on their gut feel or intuition to others.

To be effective critical thinking coaches, proven and explicit critical thinking processes are required in the three skill sets covered in this book. With that in place, the leaders' coaching role is to tap into the intrinsic motivation, self-esteem, dignity, and the curiosity and joy of learning that all of us are born with. The leaders who figure out how to harness the collective genius of the people in their organization are going to blow the competition away.

There are two elements to being effective critical thinking coaches:

- Being aware of, and managing, difficulties
- Developing appropriate questioning skills and using these skills to ask the right questions to evaluate and develop others

CRITICAL THINKING DIFFICULTIES

Human beings may regard themselves as the most intelligent creatures on the planet, but that doesn't mean they are engineered to be supreme decision makers. There has been no 1980s' Quality Movement for the human brain. The human brain was not engineered for rationality. From reckless driving behavior to gambling, from questionable mergers and acquisitions to flawed government policies, we observe irrational behavior from apparently rational, and obviously highly intelligent, people on a daily basis. Perhaps we humans think we are too smart for our own good.

More likely, it's simply that, as good as it is, our brain is not perfect, and we succumb to some common pitfalls that get in the way of effective critical thinking.

As critical thinking coaches, genuine leaders must be equipped to spot these difficulties, step in where necessary, and institutionalize systems to overcome them. The full array of pitfalls is too exhaustive to list here, so we shall limit ourselves to a few common ones and elaborate on how the critical thinking processes within this book guard against them.

CONFIRMATION BIAS

Confirmation bias is the tendency to favor information that supports personal beliefs or views. Research by Peter Watson in the 1960s implied that the de facto approach to solving problems is to confirm an existing belief, thus limiting the options considered in a decision-making scenario. Anyone who Googled "Higher driving speeds lead to increased death rates" would be exhibiting confirmation bias.

In our client work, we have seen confirmation bias manifest itself in many occasions, often in day-to-day situations such as "Decide if Susan Brown should be promoted to the vacant team leader position" or "Confirm whether Jim is the cause of low morale in the sales department."

The first example in the paragraph above is a case of a *binary decision* (with only yes or no as the options). There are many defenses against this unfavorable position of being so low in framing a decision that only one alternative is considered. The primary defense is the concept of raising the level of decision, for example, to reframe the decision objective to "Select the best team leader" for which Susan Brown is obviously one option.

The second example is a case of *framing a problem with a preengineered cause*. Poor Jim! The first critical thinking skill to apply here is one of clarification. For example, what precisely does "low morale" mean? Is it a high rate of attrition in the West Coast sales team? If so, the problem statement should be refined to be "Find the cause of the high rate of attrition in the West Coast sales team."

Jumping to conclusions is natural human behavior, but it is not critical thinking. Coach your people to avoid "gut feel" and confirmation bias!

PATH DEPENDENCE

Those above a certain age would know that the history of the QWERTY keyboard engineering design was that there was a need to distribute letters such that the arms of mechanical typewriters would not clash together. In the IT age, the QWERTY layout was extended to include a familiar array of "function keys." Thus was born the standard computer keyboard. Of course, the rationale for this design has long since been obsolete. Yet until Apple came along, the standard keyboard remained prevalent in the industry.

This use of the QWERTY keyboard design long after it was needed is an example of *path dependence*: doing things a certain way because "they've always been done that way." Apple, of course, could never throw away the core QWERTY layout, but it did make a number of subtle changes to keyboard design that others have now copied, among them, removing the function keys and adding some "free space" between the keys. With the advent of the iPad, Apple took the principle one step further with the inclusion of *context-sensitive keyboards.* For example, the @ character is not a usual inhabitant of the iPad keyboard, but bring up the e-mail application and a host of e-mail-friendly characters—@, _, and - —magically appear.

Within the Strategic Thinking Process, participants are asked to answer these questions:

- What are the current rules in your sandbox?
- Which of these rules will remain valid in the future?
- Which of these rules are obsolete or have not been questioned for a long time?

A DPI Singapore client was asked such questions as we guided the company in formulating a new strategy in the dog-eat-dog business of facilities management. Among the "rules of play" in that industry was the need to reduce fees year after year. Through the DPI process, the client created the new-to-the-market concept of *total asset management*, with the focus on maximizing facility yield. In this context, the old rule of continually reducing fees was successfully removed.

It is the leaders' responsibility to put in place the processes and thinking culture that ensure things are not done a certain way because "that's just the way it's always been done."

FRAMING BIAS

A short, simple, but effective exercise that DPI consultants like to conduct with staff members of all levels is to display a picture of a maple leaf and ask the question, "What is this?" Unsurprisingly, "A maple leaf" is the most common response! A host of perplexed faces is usually seen when the consultant replies, "Great! What is it?" "I thought we just answered that question" says the look on their faces. After a period of silence, people will typically come up with another answer: "The national symbol of Canada" they say. "Great! What is it?" comes back the reply. Then the group gets it, and the answers come flowing. The maple leaf is food, a toy, or some work to do, depending on whether you are a caterpillar, a child, or a road sweeper. The list goes on.

What this simple exercise demonstrates is that most people tend to look at a particular topic or thing from the perspective with which they are most familiar. They exhibit *framing bias.*

If something as basic as a maple leaf can be seen from at least 10 perspectives, then the business challenges faced today can be examined from a multitude of angles. The key question to ask is this: "How else can we look at this situation?"—something seasoned DPI facilitators are adept at provoking!

Innovation is an area where we've often seen framing bias raise its ugly head. Many clients see the purpose of innovation to develop products or services that will address the explicit needs of current customers. This is certainly one way to frame the purpose of innovation. However, a robust process, such as the one described in this book, would explore the topic from a multitude of angles, including these:

- Products or services based on the future needs of current customers
- Products or services based on the future needs of future customers
- New classes of customers to which existing products or services can be offered
- Innovations in the business model

TEAMS

With the increased use of teams in the workplace today, much emphasis is placed on making teams more effective. This is often described as good "teamwork."

Teams have team meetings, and meetings can be notoriously ineffective. Recently the *Times of India* caught the eye with the headline "Meetings Can Lower IQ, Make You Brain-Dead." Citing research from Virginia Tech, the article begins:

"How often do you attend meetings at your workplace? If a new research is to be believed, they can make you brain-dead, impairing your ability to think for yourself."

One of the major issues faced by teams is a lack of common language and process. Many team meetings are preoccupied by determining the meaning of key words—for example, to agree on what *strategy* is. Once that is done, the debate moves on to how to tackle the task at hand—for example, "how to craft a strategy" as opposed to actually doing it.

Another team phenomenon is *groupthink*, a term first coined by William Whyte in 1952. In groupthink, the thinking of the team regresses to the norm, as a result of peer pressure. Some classic groupthink symptoms include these:

- An air of invincibility resulting in excessive optimism and aggressive risk taking (Subprime mortgages, anyone?)
- Pressure to conform
- Shutting down of views contrary to the group consensus

Leaders that establish the terminology and processes they expect their teams to follow can eliminate redundant team meetings and reduce the likelihood of groupthink.

Fortunately, with awareness of these pitfalls, and being consciously equipped with proven thinking processes, the leader can establish a critical thinking culture that overcomes these and other difficulties.

The primary tool at the leader's disposal to do this is the capability to ask the right questions.

QUESTIONING SKILLS

The central attribute of critical thinking leaders is the ability to guide and enhance critical thinking in others. There is only one tool available to make other people think—to ask them a question.

Many leaders believe that they should know all the answers. We disagree! The job of leaders is to know the right questions to ask in order to develop others and encourage them to uncover the answers. This is a central tenet to DPI's consulting method. One role of a DPI facilitator is to ask a lot of challenging questions and let the clients come up with the answer.

Also, leaders may find themselves in a position where they are required to assess a recommendation from an individual whose discipline is different from theirs. This leads to a common dilemma: How do you evaluate the thinking of someone who knows more about a topic than you do? Our questioning techniques (specifically the notion of *process questions*) help leaders overcome this very real difficulty.

Of course, asking questions should not be at random or by chance. The pertinent question to ask about questions is what questions should be asked, when, and to whom? Any robust critical thinking process will address these questions. The ability to ask the right questions—of ourselves and others—is the essence of critical thinking.

Let's explore some lessons in questioning skills.

LESSON 1. SEQUENCE OF QUESTIONS

You wouldn't try to put the roof on a house without first building the walls. So it is with questions. It's important to ask questions in a logical sequence. A game parents play with their children is 20 Questions in which one person randomly thinks of any object and the other gets to ask up to 20 yes/no questions, after which if the questioner can correctly guess the object, he or she wins.

Younger kids will be tempted to guess at the answer straight away, but they soon realize that a better approach is to ask more general questions first and then drill down into the specifics. For example:

- Is it alive? No.
- Is it made from a material that was once alive? Yes.

- Is it made from wood? Yes.
- Is it a piece of furniture? No.
- Do you use it in sport? Yes.

The obvious point here is that the sequence of questions is important. Does it make sense to ask people what risks they see before they have determined possible causes of action? Probably not. The risks will be specific to each course of action. In *Problem Analysis* we ask questions in the order of *what*, *where*, *when*, and *how much*. This isn't by chance. It's a logical sequence. First off, the *what* must come first since if there is no *what*, the rest are simply irrelevant. Asking *how much* before *where* just doesn't seem right.

Structured and visible critical thinking processes ensure that we ask questions in a logical order and the questions are based on our understanding of where people are in their own thought process.

LESSON 2. BINARY QUESTIONS

Binary questions are questions in which the respondent must reply with one of two preordained answers, most frequently either yes or no.

As demonstrated by the game of 20 Questions, binary questions are very ineffective in gathering information. In fact, this is the only reason why 20 Questions works as a game!

Contrary to popular belief, this doesn't mean that binary questions are bad. In fact, the strengths of binary questions are in circumstances where we need to be in control or we are seeking confirmation.

Binary questions can be very useful in circumstances in which something needs to be confirmed, and they can be effectively used with paraphrasing to enhance communication. For example, "If I understood you correctly, you said that it is critically important that your new strategy manages to eliminate competitor B from your sandbox. Is that correct?"

Binary questions are also very effective when you wish to control a dialog—to steer a conversation down a desired path. For this reason, they are very popular with lawyers: "So you are the sole beneficiary of your late wife's will and have the most to gain from her murder?" Smart lawyers—at least the ones in the movies—never ask a question to which they don't know the answer, and they use binary questions to back the accused into a corner from which there is no escape.

Subtly used, binary questions can be effective in business too. It's well known that some credit cards charge a higher transaction fee than others. However, businesses still take these cards only because they cannot afford to reject such cards. These businesses would much prefer that their customers used lower transaction fee cards instead. A binary question could help these businesses. If they were to ask customers, "Would you like to pay by Visa or MasterCard?" many buyers would accede to the request, even if they have other cards in their wallet.

Despite their positive uses, from a critical thinking perspective, especially in terms of assessing the decision making of others, binary questions are of limited use, leading us to the next type of questions leaders like to ask.

LESSON 3. LEADING QUESTIONS

Leading questions influence the thinking of the recipients making it much harder for them to give an objective answer. It's hard to say what you are really thinking in response to a question worded like this: "So it seems to me that the cause of the issue is Mike. What do you think, Dave?" It is more comfortable to respond to the simpler, "What do you think, Dave?"

Leading questions are commonly used in persuasion settings, sometimes with negative impacts, especially when used prematurely. The classic presumptive close that goes along the lines of "When would you like to take delivery, Thursday or Friday?" can be very off-putting to a seasoned buyer.

Leading questions have limited use in an effective critical thinking culture. As we shall see shortly, appropriate use of process questions is far more powerful.

LESSON 4. CONTENT QUESTIONS

Content questions seek information about "things." The "thing" could be a car, an employee, a strategic plan, or a new product concept. These questions allow us to obtain and test the validity of data. Here are some examples:

- How much is it?
- How fast is it?
- When can it be ready?
- What level of education does the candidate have?

What are the risks with content questions? A few actually. First, we may be bogged down in specifics when we'd be better off thinking at a higher level. For example, our attention may be focused on the "thing" as opposed to the outcome that the "thing" is supposed to generate or what other alternatives to the "thing" exist. Second, we may not be experts about the "thing." The "thing" may be in a domain in which we have little or no experience, a phenomenon that occurs often in senior leadership positions where the staff that reports to the leader may have far superior knowledge in particular fields of expertise than the leader has.

It is very dangerous to "fight" technical or domain experts based on our cursory knowledge of the area. Alas, the mentality of "the boss must be the smartest" can often take the leader down this path.

What we need are questions that can be successfully applied regardless of the "thing," questions that enable us to validate the quality of the critical thinking of the staff reporting to us. This brings us to process questions.

LESSON 5. PROCESS QUESTIONS

Unlike content questions which are about "things," *process questions* are entirely independent of the "thing." That quality, combined with their ability to force out and make visible the thought process of others, makes them invaluable tools in the leaders' arsenal.

Through process questions, we get to understand the *how*, not the *what*. In fact, we can be totally ignorant about the *what* yet still make an informed opinion about the judgments others have made by assessing the extent to which they have applied their experience and expertise to process the information at hand.

Process questions allow us to:

- Assess the recommendations of others, one of the primary activities of management, based not on our ability to out-expertise them but by testing their logic and rationale.
- Coach others to think more critically by subtly guiding them along an appropriate thought process, without spoon-feeding them or bludgeoning them with leading questions.

One could argue that the ultimate process question is, "How did you arrive at this conclusion?" Yet this is too general to gain incisive insights into the thinking of others. The leader needs to assess the nature of the decision and then ask an appropriate series of more specific process questions in the right sequence.

Each critical thinking process comes with its own set of process questions, each designed to be used at specific points within the process. As an example, some of the major process questions of Decision Analysis are these:

- How did you develop the selection criteria for this decision?
- How do the alternatives you considered compare against these criteria?
- How have you assessed the risk of your recommendation, and how do you intend to manage that risk?

These three simple yet profound questions can be used to validate any operational or day-to-day decision regardless of the "thing" that is the topic of the decision. Next time you need to assess a recommendation of a colleague in a domain outside of your comfort zone, try these questions. They work!

SUMMARY

Leaders are not authoritarian experts whose job it is to teach people the "correct" view of reality. Rather, leaders should help everyone in the organization, themselves included, to gain more insightful views of current reality.

This requires them to bring to the surface and challenge prevailing mental models and to foster more systematic patterns of thinking.

Much of the leverage that leaders can actually exert lies in helping people achieve more accurate, more insightful, and more empowering views of reality through an appropriate use of questions.

The best leaders go one step further: they take steps to implement the necessary critical thinking processes into the fabric of their organizations. This is the topic of Chapter 14.

The Leader as Process Manager and Implementer

O ne of the interesting misconceptions that senior executives have about their job descriptions revolves around what it is they think that they manage. During our decades of collective consulting work with senior executives, we have often asked them: "What do you, as managers, 'manage'?" Their answer, 99 percent of the time, is "people."

"Not so," comes the reply!

"Oh?" they reply.

"That's right!"

"What then?" they ask.

Here's what people in organizations really manage: Middle managers manage people. Senior managers manage processes. Lower-level people manage things.

PEOPLE WHO MANAGE THINGS

These people are found at the bottom of the organization chart. They are the operators, mechanics, pipefitters, and electricians found in a manufacturing company, or the frontline executives and administrative personnel found in a white-collar area or in service industries.

These people manage things. Their role is to get things done, to get the product out the door, to service customers. Operators manage tools and production machines. Administrative people manage calculators, computers, and other gadgets to aid their productivity. They attempt to maintain these things in good working order so as to obtain the best yield and productivity. They require good content knowledge about the things that they manage.

PEOPLE WHO MANAGE PEOPLE

These individuals are found in the middle of the pyramid. They are usually referred to as *supervisors, foremen,* or *superintendents* in a manufacturing environment or as *section heads, department chiefs,* or even *directors* in a white-collar environment. They manage people because it is their role to schedule employees' time and shifts of work, handle their workloads, resolve their conflicts, and ensure that they are generally happy in their work.

These middle managers are concerned about logistics, scheduling, and relationships. They also are required to evaluate the thinking of those who work for them, for which they require the robust application of process questions.

PEOPLE WHO MANAGE PROCESSES

These people reside at the zenith of the organization. Contrary to popular belief, these senior managers are not responsible for managing other people but rather, for managing processes. Senior executives are responsible for choosing and putting into place the processes, systems, and/or methods that will get the people in an organization to behave as the organization wants.

Peter Senge in his book *The Fifth Discipline* used the analogy of an ocean liner to describe the role of senior leadership. According to Senge, most leaders see their job role as analogous to the ship's captain. Although the captain's role is obviously the most romantic and visible, the leader's perception is clearly flawed! Revered he may be for his "heroic death," but not many leaders would like to "go down with their ship" the way Captain Smith from the *Titanic* did. Fewer still would want to run aground like Captain Schettino of the *Costa Concordia*. Senge's analogy neatly demonstrates that these leaders overlooked the role of the designer of the ship. Design of the business—and its associated strategy, business model, systems, and processes—is the prerogative of the senior leaders. For this they require systems thinking.

WHICH PROCESSES

Historically the word *process* conjured up images of a production line or factory. That is, the word was most commonly used in the manufacturing sense.

More recently, *process* has acquired a wider interpretation, and professionals now frequently talk about *business* processes, *supply chain* processes, *sales* processes, *human resources* processes, *business* process outsourcing, and so on. *The one process we must never outsource is our* thinking *process!*

We have often said to clients: "If you want to change the behavior of people, put it into the *system*." These systems include the following:

- Compensation
- Planning

- Budgeting
- Product development
- Test marketing
- Auditing
- Promotion
- Performance review
- Job classification

To this list of paper or IT systems, our contention at DPI is that it is also management's responsibility to choose and put into place the *thinking* processes that they wish used in the organization:

- Strategic thinking
- Innovative thinking
- Situation management

It is these processes that are at the root of all others, and therefore they are the most critical processes of all, and the hardest to replicate when embraced fully. The familiar management refrain that "our people are our greatest asset" is only partially true. The "right" people are the greatest asset, and what determines "right" ultimately boils down to how these people think, and what they do with their thinking.

PROCESS AS THE ROOT OF CULTURE

Staff at all levels of our clients' organizations frequently tell us, "We have a different culture."

This raises the obvious follow-up question: "What is your culture?"

"We cannot describe it," they reply, "but our culture is different than our competitors' or that of the company next door."

Culture is a very difficult thing to define, but as good a definition as we have come across is that culture is simply "how things are done around here." Having heard these "We are different" statements so frequently, we decided to investigate what it is about an organization that is at the root of that organization's culture, the root of how things are done. Studying organizations to uncover the answer to this mystery proved to be a futile exercise. To obtain an answer, we need instead to investigate what is at the root of the culture of a country. Then the answer becomes evident. The root of a country's culture is that country's language. Language is the root of literature, poetry, song, opera, music, theater, humor, and so on—all the elements that make up a country's "culture."

The analogy is this: *language is to a country's culture what management processes are to an organization's culture.* Culture is the result of the processes that management chooses and uses to manage the organization. It is these processes that set the stage for how things are (or at least should be) done.

Therefore, if management wants to create a certain culture in the organization, it must choose the processes that will cause its people to behave in a manner that results in the desired culture. The culture of an organization is the result of the processes with which management chooses to manage the business. This is so because a process provides a common language that can be used to deal more effectively with business issues. Just as language is the root of a country's music, literature, and theater, so is a common thinking process the root of better decisions, strategies, and opportunities for an organization.

If management wishes to breed a culture of sound strategic thinking, it must choose the process of strategic thinking it wants its people to use. If management wishes to breed an innovative culture, then it must choose the process of innovation it wants its people to use. In other words, management's role is to select the "languages" that it wishes its people to speak while conducting business on behalf of the organization.

Management's most important responsibility is to institutionalize these processes into the organization so that they become part and parcel of its fabric and culture. However, we have found that institutionalizing *thinking* processes into an organization is easier said than done.

THE SKEW TOWARD TANGIBLE PROCESSES

Every business or organization can be broken down into three main components:

- Every business takes certain raw materials (input)
- And converts these (processes)
- Into a finished product (output)

Furthermore, everyone would agree that the quality and quantity of the output is dependent on the effectiveness of the process to convert the input into a finished product. In fact, the quality and quantity of the finished product are determined by the effectiveness of the process.

However, there are two kinds of processes in existence in any business—tangible and intangible. The *tangible processes* are the obvious ones such as manufacturing, accounting, recruiting, invoicing, compensation, and capital expenditure (Figure 14.1).

The *intangible processes* are more subtle in nature but equally important (Figure 14.2). These are the thinking processes that people use to manage business, and they are the processes we have been discussing in this book. Their input consists of the data, expertise, and experience of those using them, and the results are superior business judgments from the collective insights and "nuggets" the processes rapidly fuse together.

Most executives invest enormous amounts of money to improve their tangible processes and relatively nothing to improve the intangible ones.

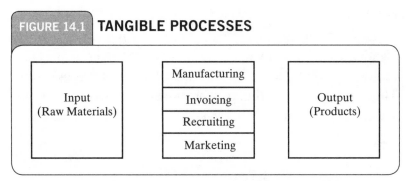

Copyright © Decision Processes International. All rights reserved.

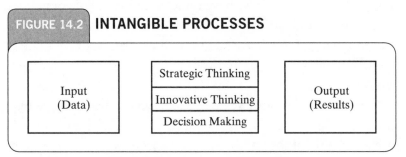

Copyright © Decision Processes International. All rights reserved.

The difficulty lies in the fact that we are not dealing with a visible system such as enterprise resource planning (ERP) software but rather, with an invisible process that occurs inside someone's head. The trick is to turn this invisible, uncoded, *soft process* into a codified, tangible tool that can be seen in *hard copy form*. As long as an organization's processes are uncodified and invisible, it will be difficult to perpetuate them and transmit them to other people. If an organization wants to be successful, it must codify its key thinking processes in order to transfer them to large groups of people and ensure their use on an ongoing basis. Process implementation, then, becomes a critical subject.

"How many such processes should we try to indoctrinate into our people?" you might ask. The answer is simple. Just as the best linguists can usually master only four or five languages, the same is true about management, or thinking, processes. No organization should attempt to use more than a few management processes if it expects its people to use and master them over time. The task of choosing thinking processes that are critical to the success of the organization is a key task of senior management.

PROCESS IMPLEMENTATION

As a result of the work we have done in thousands of companies in dozens of industries worldwide, the processes described in the previous chapters have been validated. In other words—they work. When properly used, they lead to faster and better decisions and conclusions.

However, from our 35 years' experience, what we have also noticed is that whether they work in any client organization is not a function of the validity of the concepts but rather, a function of the implementation strategy used to bring them in-house. How you bring in these concepts and processes and transmit them to people is directly related to the results you will achieve. You can obtain very good results, very poor results, or anything in between.

In response, we have developed some advice and observations that we hope would be useful to those attempting to infuse our processes into their organization (usually as a part of a culture change initiative). Failure to select the right implementation strategy will significantly and adversely impact the desired result.

KNOWN KNOWNS

Donald Rumsfeld, then U.S. secretary of defense, in his response to a journalist's question during his Defense Department briefing on February 12, 2002, made waves with his infamous "known knowns" reference: "There are known knowns; there are things we know we know. We also know there are known unknowns; that is to say, we know there are some things we do not know. But there are also unknown unknowns—there are things we do not know we don't know."

The same can be said of the stages of learning in life. A wise man explained that humanity goes through four stages of learning in life:

- Unconscious incompetent
- Conscious incompetent
- Unconscious competent
- Conscious competent

The *unconscious incompetent* is the person who is not very good at what he or she does but is not cognizant of the lack of competence. Such a person cannot be helped. When combined with an overinflated ego, this individual is a very dangerous animal!

The *conscious incompetent* is a person who is not good at what he or she does but is at least aware of that fact. This person will be receptive to help.

Unconscious competents are good at what they do, but unfortunately, they don't understand why. They are not cognizant of the specific skills they apply to achieve success. They may attribute their success to fortune or intuition. These people cannot transfer their skill to anyone else because they do not understand it themselves. A good example is the difficulty many athletes have when they try to coach others, as we described in Chapter 2.

The *conscious competent* is the best position to attain. These people excel at what they do, and they are also cognizant of the method or process that they have perfected to attain that level of skill. These people can transfer their knowledge to others. These are the "students of the game" who have analyzed the processes and habits of winning such that they can transfer the formulas to others and make them more competent.

As you have probably guessed, most managers are in the third mode—that of the unconscious competent. In other words, most managers are reasonably competent, but they do not understand the root cause of their competence. They are not aware of the processes they have subconsciously mastered that create their success. As such, they cannot transfer their skill to anyone else.

This gives rise to the *corporate learning continuum*, a straightforward yet powerful way to frame the outcome desired, and the impact and effort it will require (Figure 14.3).

The real payoff comes when senior executives take the lead to institutionalize the relevant processes into the fabric of the organization. While by no means trivial, the investment required is miniscule compared to the huge funds plowed into marquee, tangible processes and systems (such as ERP software). Furthermore, the chances of success are higher, and the results are more profound and enduring.

Let's explore the four approaches in more detail.

FIGURE 14.3 THE CORPORATE LEARNING CONTINUUM

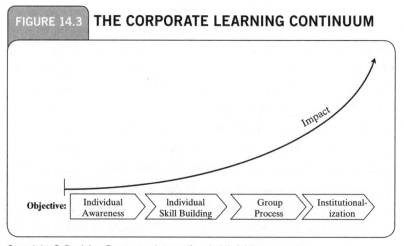

INDIVIDUAL AWARENESS

This is the first approach and the least effective. Sadly, it is the one used by most organizations.

The essence of the *individual awareness approach* is to make leaders aware of the processes they subconsciously use. This may be achieved in a three-hour session complete with presentations or exercises that enable them to see the process concepts they subconsciously apply in tangible forms.

DPI consultants have taken to calling these workshops "ah-ha" sessions. As the leaders see the processes come to life in hard copy form, they nod their heads up and down while murmuring in unison "Ah-ha, ah-ha, ah-ha."

The result is a lot of "ah-has" but not skill. Two or three hours is not enough time to build a skill. Managers may become "aware" that there are processes of thinking that can be applied to business issues, but no applicable skill can be developed around these processes in such a short period of time. This leads us to the next implementation strategy.

INDIVIDUAL SKILL BUILDING

The second possible implementation strategy is known as *individual skill building*. Its objective is to identify certain individuals who management feel would benefit from help in these skills by sending them to a two- or three-day training class.

The hope is that the individuals will come back as "born-again thinkers" and that a dramatic performance improvement in their decision-making ability will immediately occur. Some go further and expect that these born-again individuals will act as "seeds" who infuse others with their new knowledge.

Unfortunately, there are several potential problems with this approach. First, unless handled correctly, the individuals will feel as if they have a problem, especially if they are nominated to attend the workshop by HR or their manager— "Obviously my boss doesn't think I can think!" they may conclude. They may question "What's wrong with me?" that I require this "remedial" treatment.

Second, the individuals return with the full intention of using the concepts. Unfortunately, when they attempt to do so, they will find that others do not understand the concepts and lack the patience to learn them. Rather than infusing their newfound knowledge to the "ignorant" others, after a few futile attempts our born-again "process converts" will simply give up and return to their old ways. It is totally unrealistic to expect these "seeds" to overcome the corporate immune system!

Finally, repeating the first two mistakes among a large and diverse group of people leads to frustration rather than motivating the individuals involved. The whole endeavor becomes yet another "management fad of the month," and a culture of indifference is created.

For these reasons, although this approach is better than the first, most companies would be better served by moving on to the third approach.

GROUP PROCESS

This *group process approach* has a higher probability of producing better and longer-lasting results. Its objective is to identify groups of people who work together on a daily basis—often a "slice" of an organization such as a business unit or a function—and provide them with a common process to address and resolve the issues they face in the course of their work.

Naturally, the first group that must learn and use the concepts is management—the people at the top. Experience has time and again demonstrated to us that staff do what they see their bosses doing. If the leaders are seen to be active and visible practitioners and promoters of a certain process, then everyone will worship at the same altar. If the superiors are not seen as being practitioners of that process, no one will go to church. Even though significant funds may have been invested in the training of hundreds or even thousands of people in lower levels of the organization, the processes will not be used. If the processes are not seen as being good enough for the top, then they will be perceived as valueless to anyone else. Simply put, people do as you do, not do as you say!

Management must start the ball rolling by being trained in the concepts themselves and then becoming active practitioners and promoters. They must take ownership of the processes.

Once this step has been accomplished, it can be cascaded down the company.

It is important that people who participate in the group processes are from homogeneous work groups, introduced to the concepts in advance and given the opportunity to apply the concepts on the work-related issues they share. Not surprisingly, they will make significant progress on these issues while in the "training room." In fact, they will probably make more progress than if they were sitting at their desks, struggling with their "old ways."

The other requirement of this approach is that the instruction settings be *work sessions*—not training classes! And they must be conducted by *skilled facilitators*, preferably internal resources that have been trained in advance. These facilitators, over time, play two important roles.

Their first role as instructors is to conduct the work sessions and introduce people to the processes in such a manner that the tangible benefits are apparent or pointed out to all participants. A second, more important role, however, is the one the facilitators play after the initial work sessions. Most people do not master new concepts or processes in two or three days. Instead, they need access to someone who can provide additional help on the spur of the moment when they try to use the concepts but may not understand them fully. These internal facilitators can provide further counsel and assistance to the group and help it use the concepts successfully. Success breeds a desire to use the processes again and again.

These internal facilitators become invaluable assets to the organization as "process consultants." Being selected to play this role for a period of time provides tremendous personal development, and many of the facilitators will become candidates for higher-level positions.

A work session track involves at least three stages (Figure 14.4). First, there is a short and engaging *briefing session* designed to generate buy-in and prepare participants for the hands-on work sessions that will follow. Second comes an *applied workshop* in which teams learn the new processes in bite-sized chunks and immediately apply them to their real issues. Typically, 60 percent of workshop time is spent on such hands-on breakouts. Finally, there is a review four to six weeks later when necessary reinforcement takes place and further advice on execution is offered.

INSTITUTIONALIZATION

The *institutionalization approach* generates the greatest impact. It is for managers who truly value the importance of the processes and feel that these processes should be part and parcel of the corporate culture. Before you assume that the world would

FIGURE 14.4 GROUP PROCESS STRATEGY: A SYSTEMATIC IMPLEMENTATION PLAN = THE BEST RESULTS

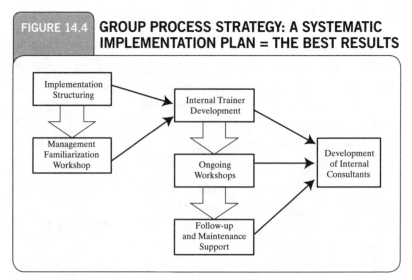

become dull if everyone became critical thinkers, please remind yourself that we are talking about the ability of an organization to succeed in a very competitive environment in which the difference between success and failure, profit and loss, winning and losing, is being just a little bit smarter than the other organization. Basically, it comes down to having a slightly better "batting average" than your competitors, an ability to score more goals than you concede. In such surroundings, doing everything you can to make your people think more logically as often as possible is well worth the investment and may produce the marginal edge you need for success.

The strategy itself is a relatively straightforward extension of the group process: over time, you incorporate the processes, or bits and pieces of them, into corporate systems and procedures. This forces the use of the processes since people are obliged to use them each time they use that particular system. After a period of time and several such repetitive uses of the system, the use of the processes will be reflexive, natural, and routine.

There are many such systems already in your organization into which our concepts can be integrated. For example, the concepts of Problem Analysis can be built into customer complaint reports and IT troubleshooting methods. The concepts of Decision Analysis can be incorporated into personnel selection and recruitment, as well as capital expenditure requests. The concepts of the Innovative Thinking Process can be used in product development systems and test marketing programs. There are many other systems and procedures in which these concepts can be incorporated to encourage their use on an ongoing basis.

However, it requires significant discipline and executive ownership. With the persistence of effort over time the concepts become part of the culture.

To summarize: the implementation process is a reflection of the organization's strategy and desired outcomes, as shown in Figure 14.5.

FIGURE 14.5 IMPLEMENTATION STRATEGY SUMMARY

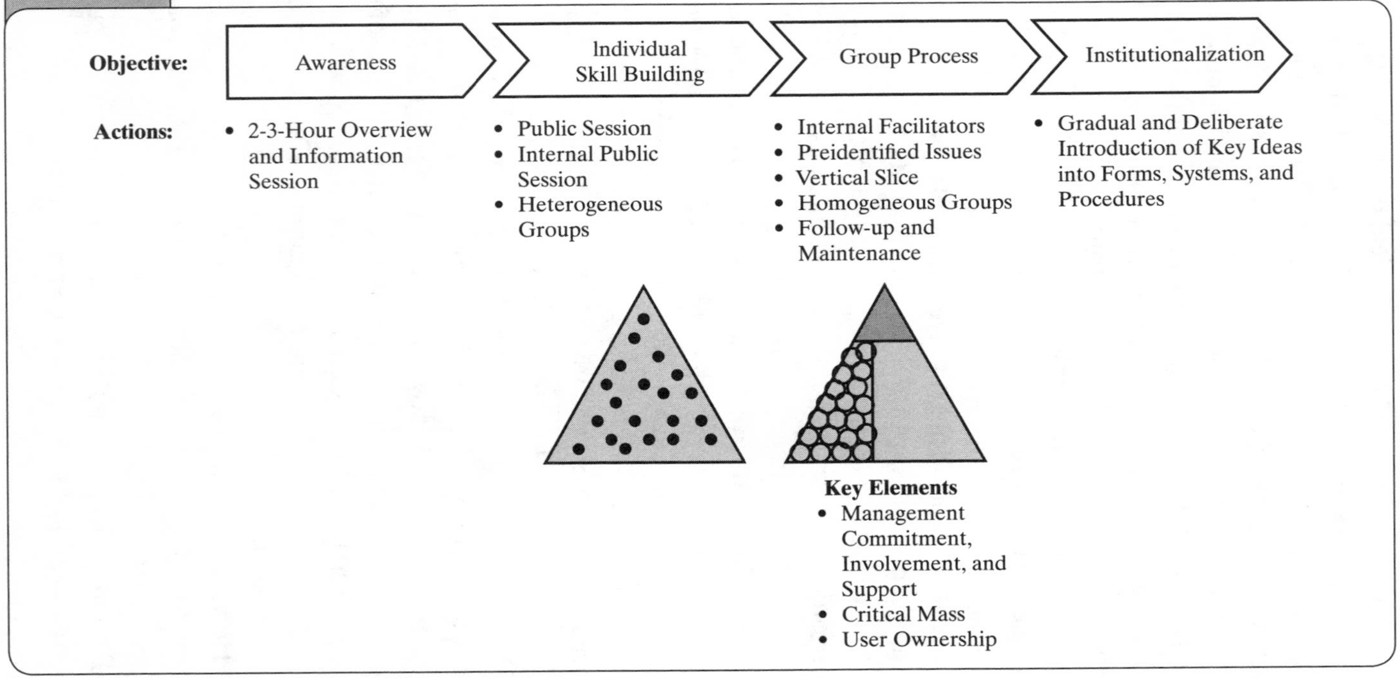

	Awareness	Individual Skill Building	Group Process	Institutionalization
Objective:				
Actions:	• 2-3-Hour Overview and Information Session	• Public Session • Internal Public Session • Heterogeneous Groups	• Internal Facilitators • Preidentified Issues • Vertical Slice • Homogeneous Groups • Follow-up and Maintenance	• Gradual and Deliberate Introduction of Key Ideas into Forms, Systems, and Procedures

Key Elements
• Management Commitment, Involvement, and Support
• Critical Mass
• User Ownership

SUMMARY

Almost everyone we know has come across the famous saying "Be careful what you ask for because you might just get it." As it turns out, this saying is highly appropriate when it comes to implementing critical thinking into your organization. An instinctive reaction to coming across a successful management approach that makes sense to leaders is for them to say, "Let's get our people trained in this." Alas, if you ask for training, that is exactly what you'll get, along with numerous cups of coffee consumed by attendees but often with largely questionable results. Instead, transformative leaders must clearly identify the end outcome they are looking for and select an appropriate method to achieve it.

PART 6

THE TRANSFORMATIONAL LEADER

CHAPTER 15

Leadership Pure and Simple

W e started this book on the premise that leadership is not a mythical trait of personality. Our firmly held view, supported by our 35 years of practical client experience, is that leadership is rooted in the ability to think critically, instill such practices in others, and engage the entire organization in critical and aligned thought in the areas of strategy, innovation, and implementation.

In the years ahead the need for critical thinking is only going to grow. The dynamics of global competition have shifted significantly, and the rate of change will continue to accelerate, resulting in tougher and rougher conditions "out there."

In the face of stiff competition from across the globe, it is tempting to cry foul and blame losses on low-cost competition, unreasonable government policies, or those playing to new and unfair rules. But that is the very nature of competition! Our view is that the losers are simply being "out-thunked." Thinking has become the lost skill of the losers.

To avoid being outwitted, decision making needs to improve at all levels, requiring systematic, creative, collective critical thinking to be pervasive in your organization. It is your role as a transformative leader to make this happen. If you can, you will already be halfway to supremacy in your chosen sandbox.

Why so? For some mysterious reason, in the majority of organizations across the globe, the processes of critical thinking have somehow avoided the "business process revolution." Peer into any firm and you will find processes for practically every aspect of its business. From production to distribution, finance to human resources management, expense claims to payroll, the need to implement systems and processes that ensure consistent, repeatable operations has become widely recognized.

Yet, as noted, there is a curious omission: in the realm of management thinking, the temptation of the quick fix seems to be too hard to resist. It is easier to turn to the nearest gurus and their latest "flavor of the month" rather than apparently harder, but certainly harder-nosed, critical thinking.

New management fads rarely deliver significant impact for the simple reason that they are usually engaging metaphors or concepts with great imagery but no "how to" supporting it. Without a process to fall back on, and their associated process questions, the natural tendency is to revert to the comfortable and familiar, especially when under pressure.

In writing this book we believe that we have made a compelling case for the position of critical thinking at the very core of leadership. Our view is that there are three explicit and fully describable critical thinking processes that underpin all effective leaders. To build a winning organization, the transformative leaders must be persuaded to take steps to master critical thinking for themselves and believe in their own capacity to implement critical thinking processes into the fabric of their organizations.

Only then can these leaders fully leverage the "number one asset" they are so fond of referring to in their missions and visions: their people. This is not a "nice to have." In the era that we are entering into, no organization on this planet can afford to be less than the very best it is capable of.

Our firm, Decision Processes International, has worked with thousands of clients across the globe over the last 35 years. Our work with people at all levels of organizations—from the CEOs, senior executives, middle managers, to even the hourly staff— has convinced us that the single greatest impediment to being a winning organization is an acute inability to think on the part of a large number of these people. This difficulty is exacerbated when issues have to be resolved in a group setting. The lack of a "common language," or critical thinking process, is seen in dramatic fashion by the large number of erroneous conclusions arrived at in all these major corporations.

These difficulties reflect themselves in people's inability to do the following:

- Separate strategic decisions from operational ones
- Separate problem issues from decision issues
- Address the causes of a problem rather than its effects
- Ensure the successful implementation of decisions by anticipating potential problems before they occur
- Distinguish between situations that require creative thinking from those that need rational analysis

Over and over, our clients and DPI have noticed that if they had a common process of thinking that could be used by groups of people trying to resolve critical issues, their conclusions and actions would be significantly better. This, to us, is leadership pure and simple. Achieving it is not as hard as it seems. It simply requires the implementation of the processes of critical thinking we have presented in this book. The result is commitment, clarity, and consensus leading to the best allocation and synchronization of limited resources to deliver measurable performance improvement. That, not their personalities, is what has made transformative leaders such as Branson, Jobs, and Welch stand out from the crowd.

People are indeed creatures of habit. Unfortunately, in business today they are creatures of bad habits—namely, the inability to think straight. In reading this book you have just taken the first step to correct this. Good luck!

INDEX

ABOUT THE AUTHORS

David Wilkins is the managing partner of DPI Singapore and works with clients across Asia to help them improve the quality of their strategic and operational decisions. He spearheads the development and enhancement of the company's Strategy Execution Framework and Situation Management Processes.

Greg Carolin is the managing partner of DPI Africa and has extensive experience working with organizations across a variety of industries in South Africa and the United Kingdom, helping them improve the quality of their critical business decisions. He focuses on the ongoing development of all the company's Critical Thinking Processes for application across industries.